The History of

Pangrati

Kalavryta, Peloponnese,

Greece

Παγκράτι

Καλάβρυτα, Πελοπόννησος, Ελλάδα

To Cindy,
Thank you for for support.
Enjoy the book.
Ted
Theodore P Corry

Valuable and fascinating story of the small village of Pangrati in the mountains of southern Greece. The reader can vicariously walk through the village during times of oppression and war, in both happy and sad times. Incredibly well researched using sources in numerous languages. This book will be especially meaningful to English language readers who desire to learn about this small but important village. As the local Association of this village, it is important to keep our history and heritage alive especially for the future generations. Bravo, Theodore Georgas for collecting and documenting the history of not only the village but the region and its traditions!

Συλλογοσ Παγκρατιωτων Καλαβρυτινων

Pangrati Kalavryton Association

Map of the Peloponnese of Greece from 1827 that shows my grandparents ancestral home, the village of Pangrati (labeled Pangradi). This proves that the village is nearly 200 years old.

Published in Cenni statistici sulla Morea con carta geografica. Milano: Presso gli Editori degli Annali universali delle scienze e dell'industria.

English Translation: Published in Statistical notes on Morea with geographical map. Milan: At the Publishers of the Universal Annals of Sciences and Industry.

The History of Pangrati

Kalavryta, Peloponnese, Greece

Παγκράτι

Καλάβρυτα, Πελοπόννησος, Ελλάδα

By Theodore P. Georgas

© Copyright 2019 Theodore P. Georgas

ISBN: 978-0-578-61032-0

Published by

Theodore P. Georgas

In loving memory of

Theodore Nicholas Georgas

and

Veneta Vlangos Georgas

Table of Contents

Acronyms and Terms

aka   also known as

BLO   British liaison officer

ca.   circa

EA   National Solidarity (Greek: Εθνική Αλληλεγγύη) was the social welfare organization of the EAM Resistance movement in occupied Greece during World War II.

EAM   National Liberation Front (Greek: Εθνικό Απελευθερωτικό Μέτωπο; romanized: Ethniko Apeleftherotiko Metopo) was the main movement of the Greek Resistance during the Axis occupation of Greece.

ELAS   (ΕΛΑΣ) Greek People's Liberation Army (Greek: Ελληνικός Λαϊκός Απελευθερωτικός Στρατός; romanized: Ellinikós Laïkós Apeleftherotikós Stratós), often mistakenly called the National People's Liberation Army, was the military arm of the left-wing National Liberation Front (EAM) during the period of the Greek Resistance.

EPON   (ΕΠΟΝ) The United Panhellenic Organization of Youth (Greek: Ενιαία Πανελλαδική Οργάνωση Νέων) was a Greek Resistance organization that was active during the Axis occupation of Greece in World War II. EPON was the youth wing of the National Liberation Front (EAM).

SOE   Special Operations Executive

SS   Abbreviation of Schutzstaffel (German: "Protective Echelon"), the black-uniformed elite corps and self-described "political soldiers" of the Nazi Party. Founded by Adolf Hitler in April 1925 as a small personal bodyguard, the SS grew with the success of the Nazi movement and, gathering immense police and military powers, became virtually a state within a state.[1]

---

[1] https://www.britannica.com/topic/SS

Pangrati in Ancient Times

Photo of Pangrati, Greece, that I took in 1992.

The Greek village known as Pangrati (aka Pagrati) dates back to at least the year 1700. The Venetians, the rulers at the time, carried out a census of the villages, including Pangrati, in what was then known as Morea.

Pangrati is located on a mountain in the Peloponnese, a peninsula in southern Greece. The elevation of the village is approximately 2800 feet (850 m) above sea level. This is quite high, considering the sea is only 40–50 miles (64–80 km) away in two directions, north and southeast. The region around Pangrati was first inhabited in the Paleolithic Period (about 100,000 years BC), and the first Greek civilizations began around 2000 BC. The main settlement of the ancient Greeks, and the center of their world, was Mycenae, which was 31 miles (50 km) southeast of Pangrati. The Mycenaeans were famously written about by

Homer: *The Iliad* tells of King Agamemnon ruling Mycenae. The exact dates of his rule are unknown, but experts believe it could be anywhere from the 16th to 11th century BC.

The area of northern Peloponnese, where Pangrati is located, was inhabited by the Achaean tribe. According to Pausanias, a second century Greek geographer, the people known as Achaeans were so named because they were descended from the sons of the mythical Achaeus: Archander and Architeles.[2] The Achaeans were one of the original four major tribes of the Hellenic World. The others were the Aeolians, the Ionians and the Dorians.

The Dorians forced the Achaeans to leave the Peloponnese and move to other lands. The Dorians came from northern Greece and traveled southward into central Greece. At the end of the Bronze Age, about 1200 BC, they began migrating into the Peloponnese. The Dorians could be identified by their strong dialect and their burning desire for war. They invented the iron sword, which they used to conquer their enemies.

The Dorians conquered the last members of the Minoan and Mycenaean civilizations who were living in the southern part of Greece. Their rule plunged the area into a dark age. It took almost three centuries for the Greek city-states to emerge from Dorian dominance.

According to at least one map in ancient times the Aeolians inhabited the northern half of the Peloponnese which included all of Arcadia.[3]

---

[2] https://en.wikipedia.org/wiki/Achaeans_(tribe)
[3] Paul Vidal-Lablache, "Atlas général Vidal-Lablache 1894 - Histoire et géographie."

Map of ancient Greece - General Atlas Vidal-Lablache 1894
History and Geography.

The language spoken in Arcadia prior to the Dorian invasion was Arcado-Cypriot Greek. This was a Greek dialect that was spoken in Arcadia and also in Cyprus. According to Pausanias:

> Agapenor, the son of Ancaeus, the son of Lycurgus, who was king after Echemus, led the Arcadians to Troy. After the capture of Troy the storm that overtook the Greeks on their return home carried Agapenor and the Arcadian fleet to Cyprus, and so Agapenor became the founder of Paphos, and built the sanctuary of Aphrodite at Palaepaphos (Old Paphos).[4] [5]

---

[4] https://en.wikipedia.org/wiki/Arcadocypriot_Greek
[5] W.H.S. Jones Litt.D., and H.A. Ormerod, "Pausanias. Pausanias Description of Greece with an English Translation, in 4 Volumes." Cambridge, MA, Harvard University Press; London, William Heinemann Ltd. 1918.

After the fall of the Mycenean civilization the Arcadians and Cypriots dialects began drifting apart.

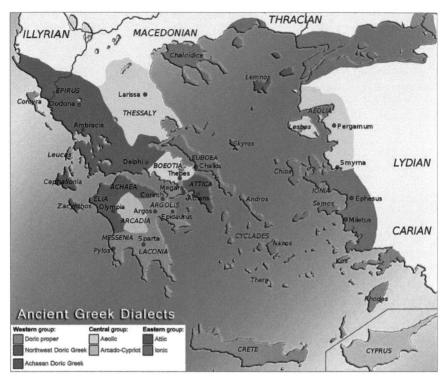

Roger D. Woodard (2008), "Greek dialects", in:
The Ancient Languages of Europe, ed. Roger D. Woodard,
Cambridge: Cambridge University Press, p.51.

Between 800 and 500 BC the ancient Greeks built the cities of Korinthos, Argos, Sparta, Mantineia and Orchomenus. All of these City-States as they were known were close to the present location of Pangrati, especially Mantineia and Orchomenus. In 776 BC the Olympic Games began. They were held every four years in Olympia, which is 34 miles (55 km) west of Pangrati. The athletes came from all over the Greek world to compete in events such as the pentathlon, which consisted of a jumping event, discus and javelin throws, a foot race and wrestling. The participants also competed in boxing, wrestling, pankration and equestrian events.

The village of Pangrati was possibly named for the Olympian sport of pankration. Perhaps some of the best athletes in the sport of pankration came from that village. The fact that the village and the violent sport had a similar name may be why the fighters of Pangrati were known for being especially fierce.

Pankration, which translates to "all force," is a combination of wrestling and boxing. It was a dangerous sport often resulting in the death of one of the combatants. The rules allowed nearly any kind of fighting, but you had no weapons except your hands, arms and legs. The only actions not allowed were biting; gouging; sticking a finger into your opponent's eye, nose or mouth; and attacking the genitals.

Pankration was one of the most popular combat sports in ancient Greece. The name *pankration* derived from the ancient Greek words for "pan" and "state," which implied that the winner of the sport was the one who had complete power over, and control of, his foes. The participants were called pankratiasts.[6]

---

[6] Theodoros Karasavvas, "Pankration: A Deadly Martial Art Form from Ancient Greece," *Ancient Origins: Reconstructing the Story of Humanity's Past*, January 23, 2016; http://www.ancient-origins.net/history-ancient-traditions/pankration-deadly-martial-art-form-ancient-greece-005221.

Pankration was introduced at the 33rd Olympics in 648 BC. "It impressed the crowds immediately because it was more diverse and exciting than any other combat sport they had seen."[7]

Pankration match circa 500 BC.
The man on the ground is signaling that he is surrendering.
The referee is getting involved with a stick to end the match.
Source: Faculty of Arts – Department of Ancient History BELGIUM:
http://ancientolympics.arts.kuleuven.be/picEN/slides/P0013.jpg.html

Theodoros Karasavvas describes this deadly martial art as follows:

> Despite offering an exciting and spectacular show to the fans who loved violence and blood, many times it could become extremely dangerous for the pankratiasts and there are several recorded

---

[7] Karasavvas, "Pankration."

cases in which the fight resulted in severe injuries, or even death, to one of the opponents—usually the one who was losing and refused to surrender. For that reason, and as most Greek city-states were becoming more sophisticated and civilized, the men's pankration was gradually replaced by the pankration for boys, which was a much less intense version of the sport. This version officially entered the Games in 200 BC.[8]

Centuries later the region that included Pangrati was invaded numerous times:

1. ***Philip II*** of Macedonia invaded in 338 BC, which led to creation of the League of Corinth.[9]

2. ***Romans*** attacked in 146 BC.[10] Pangrati was part of the Achaean League at that time.

3. ***Franks*** invaded in 1209 AD. The Barony of Kalavryta was a medieval Frankish fiefdom of the Principality of Achaea. It was located in the Peloponnese peninsula in Greece and centered on the town of Kalavryta. This barony was one of 12 in Archaea. To watch over the Greeks and maintain control the Franks built numerous castles and towers. The remains of some of these can still be seen today.

---

[8] Karasavvas, "Pankration."

[9] Rodgers, Nigel. *The Illustrated Encyclopedia of Ancient Greece: An Authoritative Account of Greek Military and Political Power, Architecture, Sculpture, Art, Drama and Philosophy*. Leicester: Anness Publishing: 2017.

[10] Ibidem.

4.   ***Turks (aka Ottoman Empire)*** invaded and took over most
       of Greece, including the Peloponnese, around 1460.
       Although many mountain villages and possibly Pangrati
       were said to have never been fully under Turkish rule, I
       find this rather hard to believe, as the entire country and
       especially the whole region around Pangrati were ruled
       by the Turks for 300 years. It seems very likely they were
       at least affected by the ruling government. Even so, the
       Turks did allow local Greeks to keep their own customs,
       language and religion. It is a well-known fact that the
       Turks allowed the nations under their rule to operate the
       country and inhabitants under their own systems of
       government and religious beliefs. In this "millet" system,
       Greece ruled itself under its own courts of law. The
       Greek Orthodox Church became even stronger and more
       powerful during Turkish rule.

5.   ***Venetians*** were present in the area for only 30 years
       (1687–1715). Venetian rule came about as a result of the
       Morean War, during which Captain-General Francesco
       Morosini and the Venetian forces destroyed much of the
       ancient Greek infrastructure, including the Parthenon in
       Athens. The Venetians fought against the Ottomans all
       over the whole world as it was known at that time,
       including the Peloponnese, with the Venetians winning
       decisive battles. Morosini was made Doge of Venice for
       his efforts to win the war and take over much of Greece.
       The Venetians were the first rulers to document the
       village of Pangrati when they took a census of all of the
       villages under their control. Thus, the first known date of
       the existence of the village of Pangrati is the year 1700.

6. The **Ottoman Empire** overtook the area once again in 1715 and ruled until 1827. On October 20, 1827, the famous sea Battle of Navarino ended the Ottoman reign and occupation of the Peloponnese. Greece was finally able to become an independent nation.

7. **Italians** with the help of the Germans and Bulgarians, invaded and occupied most of Greece including all of the Peloponnese from 1941 until 1943, during World War II.

8. **Germans** took over the occupation of Greece after Italy fell to the allied forces in 1943 and maintained control until the end of World War II in 1945.

Pangrati is part of Kalavryta Province. In ancient times, Kalavryta Province belonged to Arcadia which was a part of Azania,[11] but in 1687, after the conquest of the Peloponnese by the Venetian Morosini, it was incorporated in Achaia Prefecture, where it remains today. Azania was a region in ancient Arcadia, which was according to Pausanias named after the mythical king Azan.

> In Greek mythology Azan was the son of Arcas of Arcadia and Erato who was a Dryad, a tree nymph or human-tree hybrid. Azan was brother of Apheidas, Elatus and Hyperippe. Azania in Arcadia was named after him. He was the father of Cleitor and Coronis, mother of Asclepius by the famous god Apollo. When Azan died, the first funeral games in history were held in his honor. It was at these games that Aetolus accidentally killed Apis.

---

[11] Pausanias's Description of Greece: Commentary on books VI-VIII: Elis, Achaia, Arcadia; Macmillan, 1898 - Greece

Arcas was the son of Zeus and Callisto. Arcas was a hunter who became king of Arcadia. He was remembered for having taught people the arts of weaving and baking bread.[12] [13]

Throughout early history the area now known as Pangrati did not exist as a village, according to ancient maps. This is not a big surprise, as most inhabitants of the Peloponnese lived in towns along the sea. The sea brought goods from other ports. It provided fish to eat and had a mild climate. The perimeter of the Peloponnese was a more desirable place to live for most people. The mountains provided a much more difficult life. Winters were bitterly cold, food was harder to come by, and virtually no traders came to sell their goods. The majority of the Peloponnese residents lived near the cities so that they could work together to defend themselves against invaders. They built fortresses in all the perimeter cities, such as Argos, Corinth, Elis, Patras, Kalamata and Nafplio. It wasn't until the Middle Ages that the people of the Peloponnese (which was still referred to as Morea) started building inland towns and villages. These towns and villages were close to rivers and along routes created for transporting and trading goods. The last place people wanted to live was on the side of a high mountain, such as where Pangrati would eventually be settled. However, as more and more battles were fought over the coastal areas more people wanted to get far away from the dangers inherent in living on the front lines. They never knew when another invader would choose to strike against the city they lived in or near. Slowly, a few people started settling the lands at higher altitudes and in more remote regions. The remote location of Pangrati protected

---

[12] https://en.wikipedia.org/wiki/Azan_(mythology)
[13] https://en.wikipedia.org/wiki/Arcas

it from invaders for many centuries. That all changed when Adolf Hitler took power in Nazi Germany. Hitler and the Germans saw the mountains of the Peloponnese as very important in their overall goals of conquering Europe, North Africa and western Asia.

Location of Pangrati

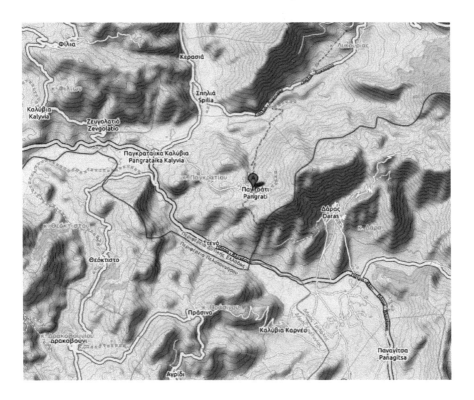

Courtesy of ACME Pangrati Terrain Map.

The village of Pangrati is at the top of a mountain and about a one-hour drive from Kalavryta. Pangrati consists of three "suburbs": Steno, Pagrateika Kalyvia, and Stella. The suburbs were all created in fertile fields near the rivers. Pangrati residents moved down from the mountains to be closer to the more fertile fields, rivers and the highway, which offered better employment opportunities as well.

World War II

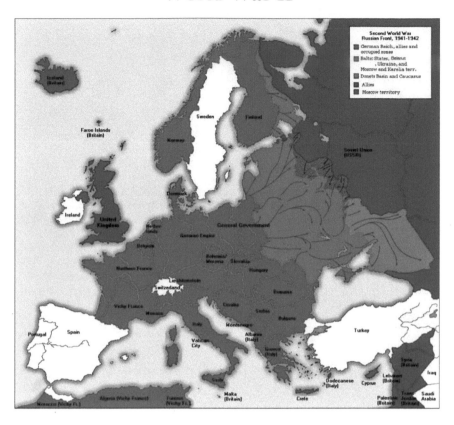

Map of Europe showing areas controlled by Axis powers Germany and Italy (in blue) in 1941-2. [14] Note that the Peloponnese of Greece is at the south end of the Axis occupation.

The village of Pangrati was strategically located just off the road between Tripoli and Kalavryta, two very important cities during World War II. These cities were most strategically located because of their central location in the Peloponnese. In 1941 the Axis powers had invaded Greece and were now occupying all of the country, including the entire Peloponnese.

---

[14] https://commons.wikimedia.org/wiki/File:Second_world_war_europe_1941-1942_map_en.png

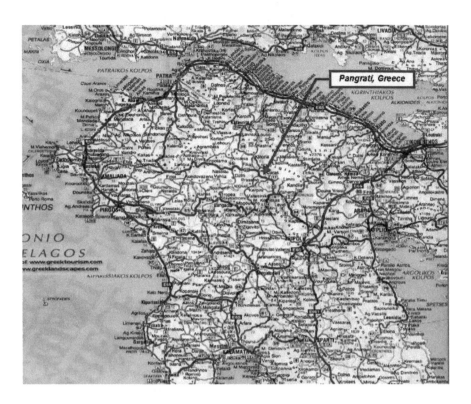

Pangrati is in the center of the Peloponnese.

Some might think that Pangrati was far removed from the war that was taking place all across Europe and northern Africa. However, Italy was united with Germany and Japan in the quest to take over the world, including Greece. The Italian army made their local headquarters in Tripoli, about 30 miles (48 km) south of Pangrati. They also had an office and an army unit in Mazeika (Μαζέικα, now the town of Kleitoria) about 6 miles (more than 9 km) north of Pangrati.

Being under the rule of a suppressive country was nothing new to the local Pangratians. They had been ruled for more than 300 years by the hated Turks and had also been under the rule of Macedonians, Romans, Franks, and Venetians for another 1700 years. By 1941 they had been a free country for over 100 years, after 2000 years of oppression, and they were not about to let the Italians or Germans rule over them. The men of the village and surrounding villages began to organize a rebellion that would make trouble for the Italians. Then Germany, realizing that the Italians were not really in complete control of Greece,

Priest Germanos III blessing the Greek flag at the monastery Agia Lavra.

started sending in its own army to suppress any Greeks that were fighting back. The larger town of Kalavryta, which is about 20 miles (32 km) north of Pangrati, was also getting organized to fight the German and Italian armies. According to some historians, Pangrati was not just a little village: it was the local supply center for the rebellion. Many of the exiled Greek leaders came through the area and helped to inspire the Resistance against the Italians and Germans that were occupying Greece.

It was near Kalavryta that the famous Agia Lavra monastery was, and still is, located. Agia Lavra was the spot were the most important Greek leaders met in early 1821 to discuss the problems they were having under Turkish rule. The Turks had treated the Greeks so badly and by 1820 were killing Greek leaders they thought might cause them problems. The leaders were mostly monks and other religious leaders of the Greek Orthodox churches. These leaders met at Agia Lavra after the Turks had demanded that the Greek leaders turn themselves in to Turkish authorities. The Greek leaders knew that if they turned themselves in, they would probably be executed. The Turks wanted to quash any thoughts of the Greeks revolting before they got started. But this actually backfired on the Turks. Some of the Greek leaders chose instead to take action against the oppressors. They resolved to strike against the Turks, now or never, kill or be killed. They had waited nearly 400 years to fight for their freedom. Some of the other Greek leaders wanted to wait and go into hiding from the Turks so they wouldn't be captured, but this wasn't a real solution. The leaders in favor of fighting figured if they were going to die at the hands of the Turks they might as well start a rebellion and get rid of them once and for all. This was a very difficult decision for some of the Greeks, as they had become good friends with some of the Turks and didn't want to start a war with them. One of the main characters in these debates was a powerful priest of Patras named Germanos III (Georgios Gotzias). He is said to have blessed the Greek flag on March 25, 1821, and thus approved and inspired the revolt.

Historians debate whether the Greek holy leaders that met at Kalavryta in early 1821 actually agreed on fighting the Turks or whether Germanos was even in favor of it. He may have actually taken credit for instigating the fighting only after the revolt succeeded. But the local Greeks did think that the holy leaders were finally endorsing the rebellion they had long desired. The result was that the Greeks who lived in the region, including Pangrati, joined forces and began fighting, which ultimately led to the freedom of the Greeks. The Turks were either killed or sent out of Greece, and the new independence led to the formation of the country of Greece. Local Greeks were very proud that they had started the rebellion that freed their lands at last from the hated Turks.

When the Greeks in the Pangrati region were taken over by the Italians in World War II, they were not about to let the Italians rule over them. The Greeks began organizing small groups that would go out at night and sabotage whatever they could to hamper the Italian forces. During the day they looked like ordinary farmers, but at night they were stealing weapons and supplies from the Italians.

Pangrati is in the Aroania Mountains
(background aerial created by Google).

The local monasteries housed priests that preached against the foreign aggressors and were stirring emotions in the local Greeks to rise up once again as their ancestors had when they ignited the revolt that sent the Turks back to their own country in 1821. The Italians were Roman Catholic, and the Germans were persecuting anyone that was not Aryan German. The Greeks wanted to keep their precious Orthodox religious practices intact. Their religious beliefs and daily rituals were vital to their way of life and were to be kept at all costs. After all, they did not have much else in life. They were mostly poor farmers or goat and sheep herders.

The Greeks' only real liberty in life was their choice to believe in the Holy Spirit, and for that they listened intently to the monks in the monasteries. Their deeply founded religious beliefs are still seen today: nearly every village, no matter how large or small, has its own church.

Sheep and goats are a common sight in and around Pangrati.

The monasteries had been able to keep the real Orthodox ways alive through 2000 years of foreign rule and didn't let the Germans or the Catholics tell them that their ways were no longer acceptable and must be destroyed. They pushed the local population to organize and rise up to fight the foreign invaders. Similar uprisings all across Greece were inspired by Greek heritage, culture, religion and pride.

In addition, the British had sent to the Pangrati area a few select military operatives to help the Greek Resistance movement. For strategic purposes the bridges on the two rivers that flowed right next to Pangrati were essential for the Italians and later on the German armies for moving their troops around the area.

In efforts to support advances in southern Europe and northern Africa, the German army, led by Adolf Hitler, desperately needed to move large volumes of supplies from Germany straight south through Europe and Greece to the Mediterranean Sea. From there they could move men, equipment and supplies to points all over the various war fronts. The fighting in Africa and Russia was especially important to Germany and its Axis co-aggressors in their attempt to win the war. The main route the Germans selected to move everything was literally right through Pangrati.

The Pangratians and others in the region joined up as Resistance fighters. They demolished the bridges to curtail enemy movements. They ripped up the roads and installed roadblocks. The Greek Resistance fighters had no need for the bridges, since they did not have any vehicles. The rivers were not very deep and could easily be crossed by foot except during high flows in the spring, when the snow was melting from the surrounding mountains. Local Greeks had gotten around for centuries without bridges, and they did anything they could do to help their allies win the war and preserve the Greek culture.

Early in the war, the Italians frequently needed to move between Mazeika and Tripoli along the road through Pangrati. The Italian army came to Pangrati and saw the bridges had been destroyed. They expressed their anger toward the people of Pangrati and said they were going to kill them al. But the Italians had a change of heart, as they needed the bridges rebuilt. So, they forced the Pangratians to rebuild the bridges but told them they would still kill them after they were done. When the bridges were rebuilt, the Italians changed their minds once again and let the Pangratians live. This shows that the Italians were not really out to make the Greeks suffer and that not every

Italian soldier hated the Greeks. In fact, many Italians thought of the Greeks as closer to them in race than they did to their own allies, the Germans. The average Italian soldier felt sympathetic to the Greek plight. Most Italian soldiers just wanted to serve their time in the army with as little conflict as possible and then return to their own homes. But there were Italian military leaders that were under pressure from Mussolini that hated the Greeks and treated them horribly. Consequently, they stole everything they could from the local Greeks. They tried beating and torturing them, even to the point of executing some to get all of them under control. But the Italians were never really able to get full control of the Greeks.

Hitler thought the Italians should handle everything in southern Europe. But the Italian soldiers had been doing a horrible job, as far as Hitler was concerned. The Italians seemed to fail at every military endeavor. In Pangrati they could not control a few pesky Greek farmers. The Germans decided they would have to handle the Greeks themselves.

Things in the region got much more serious after the Germans sent the Italian armies home and took over securing Greece with their own forces. Once again, the local Greeks in the area around Pangrati and especially Kalavryta were the chief instigators of trouble for the Germans. The German leaders were very much aware of the local Greeks that were forming as bands of Resistance fighters in the mountains around Kalavryta. The leaders sent in troops in a sweeping movement to squash the Resistance, as it was preventing the movement of German troops and supplies through the region. Using informants, the Germans searched everywhere for the Resistance leaders. After hearing that the Resistance was located in or near the village of

Rogoi, just north of Kalavryta, the Germans decided to attack. The Battle of Kerpini, as it was known as, was fiercely fought on both sides, but the Germans were not prepared for how well the Greeks fought. They thought the Greeks fighters were simple farmers who knew nothing of modern warfare. And the German troops were well trained. But the Germans underestimated the Greeks and ended up getting captured after they were forced to surrender. The Greeks took into custody about 80 German soldiers, but they were totally unprepared to handle prisoners, especially so many. Three of the Germans were left behind so the Greeks could treat their wounds. The remaining German soldiers were transported to Mazeika, where they were detained for a while. The Greeks tried to negotiate their release with the German leaders. In exchange, they wanted many Greeks released who had been captured by the Germans. The Germans refused to negotiate. The Greeks took the German captives to a mountain near Planitero, where they forced them to jump off a high cliff to their death. The Greeks did not have much choice—they had no prison to hold the captives. And holding them would have been very dangerous. Letting them go would have been even more dangerous. So, they killed them in hopes of securing their region from the invaders. At the time they thought this was a great victory for Greece. They had successfully defeated a large German combat group. This was looked at as a huge accomplishment for the Andartes (Greek Resistance fighters), who were really just peasant farmers.

This cliff was in a very remote area deep in the mountains, and the Greeks thought the German leaders would not find out that their soldiers had been murdered. But that didn't work out: word of the killings spread. And after a while even Hitler himself learned of this event.

The event was big news across Europe. Hitler didn't want to have to fight another front line of enemies. He had his hands full fighting the French and British to his west, the Russians to his east, and the Americans in Africa. He decided to take aggressive action to stamp out the Greek Resistance movement in the Peloponnese once and for all. He turned to his most ruthless military commander and told him to go to the Kalavryta region, which included Pangrati, and destroy the Greeks. He wanted 100 dead Greeks for every killed German soldier, 8000 Greeks for the 80 Germans. But more on this story later.

Battle of Kerpini on October 17, 1943

Here is how the Kerpini (Rogoi) battle unfolded, according to Hermann Frank Meyer in his book *From Vienna to Kalavryta* (as interpreted from the German by Theodore P. Georgas):[15]

> Andartes led by Nikos Nikolopoulos—known as the Nikitas attack—came as a surprise to Hauptmann Johannes Schober. As if lying on a presentation platter, the Germans were attacked from three sides with rifles and machine guns. Nevertheless, Schober succeeded in returning his men to the shelter of a narrow, tree-covered side valley. After dark, Schober moved his troops quickly to a higher altitude, where he maneuvered into a hedgehog defensive position and fended off further Andartes attacks during the night.
>
> On the night of October 16th, Schober's company was now on a hill that separated Kerpini from Kalavryta. He regretted his decision to not bring a radio with him, because he was unable to summon reinforcements.
>
> The Kalavryta–Andartes forces were determined to use all means to prevent the Germans from entering and destroying their city. Of course, they had no way of knowing that the Germans were only operating a reconnaissance mission and not

[15] Hermann Frank Meyer, *Von Wien nach Kalavryta: Die blutige Spur der 117, Jäger-Division durch Serbien und Greichenland* (Mannheim: Peleus, 2002) [*From Vienna to Kalavryta: The Bloodstained Trail of the 117th Jaeger Division through Serbia and Greece*, as translated from the German by Theodore P. Georgas.]

intending to occupy Kalavryta. A former Andarte, Filipos Zissimopoulos, who was a hairdresser in Kalavryta in civilian life, remembered how during the night Andartes runners were sent to Vissoka, Valtsa and Kalavryta to mobilize reinforcements. In fact, the members of the so-called reserve ELAS (the Greek People's Liberation Army) and the peasants of the surrounding villages left their plows, left their animals in the stables, brought out their old weapons, and gathered at night, in the tradition of their forefathers, to meet the occupier head on. Even eight patients lying in the Kalavryta hospital joined forces to fight. "Overall, we increased by more than 200 men during the night," recalls Zissimopoulos.

Schober did not dare to go down to Kalavryta to call in reinforcements over the public telephone network, as he did not know whether the city was occupied by Andartes. So that night he decided to break through at dawn to the northwest, to reach the west of Kerpini in a northern direction to Aigio.

This attempt was made at exactly four o'clock in the morning of October 17th. Heavy, eventful battles lasted throughout the day, resulting in casualties on both sides. Essential parts of the company managed to get up to 650 feet (200 m) below a high saddle by the evening. From this location the descent toward Digela, about 1 mile (1.6 km) north of Kerpini, would have been possible.

German soldier Alois Pühringer (who would later be awarded the German Cross for bravery)[16] remembers, "We all walked around in a rather depressed state of mind." Schober had observed how Pühringer had "eaten his chicken meat out of the dishes and then drunk everything out of the bottle of Oberjäger [head soldier] Ratzenböck." This, according to Pühringer, had caused Ratzenböck, who in this desperate situation waited in vain for Schober's orders, to insult Schober with expressions like "Herr Hauptmann, Sie sind ein Schwein" ("Captain, you are a pig"). It seems that Schober stayed motionless as he accepted these insults and in this highly explosive situation was unable to command and take the appropriate action.[17]

According to the Irish agent Conal O'Donnell, who was nearby at the time,

> On October 17, 1943 communist ELAS partisans captured 81 German soldiers from I Battalion 749 Jaeger Regiment of the 117th Jaeger Division near Kalavryta. The men were not first rate troops, but should have been able to shoot their way out of the ambush on a mountain track near the villages of Kerpini and Rogoi. Many were Austrians, with a few Alsatians [men from the Alsace-Lorraine region of France] and other conscripts from occupied Europe. The rest were German. The unit

---

[16] Foundation for Information on World War Two, "Deutsches Kreuz in Gold," *Traces of War*, https://www.tracesofwar.com/awards/614/Deutsches-Kreuz-in-Gold.htm?sort=name&show=list&abc=P&page=2

[17] Meyer, *From Vienna to Kalavryta* (translated from the German by Theodore P. Georgas).

was commanded by Hauptmann Johannes Schober.[18]

Eleven Germans were able to escape the trap they were in and get out to the northwest to go back toward Aigio. The next day they got back to base camp and reported what had happened. At first the Germans offices in the camp did not believe them, for they were badly disoriented and talking nonsensically.

Hermann Frank Meyer, in his book *From Vienna to Kalavryta* (as interpreted from the German by the Theodore P. Georgas), had this to add:[19]

> There are varying statements about the losses in the battle at Kerpini, but it seems certain that nine Greeks and four Germans were killed.
>
> A few days later, when Major Ebersberger (Schober's commander) had the "battle tracks" analyzed, he was astonished at the "minor bloody losses" of his company, especially since the "ammunition effort of the enemy" had been very high. Ebersberger guessed the reason was the "bad shooting performance of the opponent." This was not surprising, given that some of these spontaneous farmers fought with antiquated weapons and had no military training comparable to that of the German soldiers.

---

[18] Conal O'Donnell, "SOE, the Irish Agent and the Greek Massacre," *WW2 People's War*, http://www.bbc.co.uk/history/ww2peopleswar/stories/37/a3206837.shtml
[19] Meyer, *From Vienna to Kalavryta* (translated from the German by Theodore P. Georgas).

From the German point of view, Ebersberger drew the devastating conclusion in the days following the disaster that there was "no antidote" to the Andartes. In northwestern Peloponnese, they were dealing with a "numerically strong, well-organized and well-armed gang," which had a good observation system and rapid messaging and was very agile. Enlightenment actions, such as those carried out by Schober, "are useless."[20]

On the evening of October 17, the German occupiers returned to Kalavryta, not as conquerors but surprisingly as prisoners of the ELAS /Andartes. And it wasn't just one or two German soldiers, but a whole company.

Among the prisoners were three soldiers who had been wounded during the battle. They were admitted to the Kalavryta hospital, while a fourth German, who had suffered a life-threatening pulmonary attack and was unable to be transported, had been left by the Andartes in the care of Kerpini's doctor.

For the next seven weeks the Greeks held the 78 German soldiers as prisoners, moving them from place to place to avoid the German army, which was looking for them. They were taken from the battlefield to Kerpini, then to Kalavryta, where they were imprisoned in the school. When the Kalavrytans heard that the Germans were searching for their missing men and heading toward Kalavryta, they decided to move the prisoners to Mazeika. On the way they stopped at the famous monastery Agia Lavra. This is where the Germans leaders, especially Hans

---

[20] Meyer, *From Vienna to Kalavryta* (translated from the German by Theodore P. Georgas).

Schober, were interrogated by a British agent with the permission of the ELAS/Andartes who had captured them. The British agent is said to have advised the ELAS to release the prisoners so they would not provoke a violent response from the Germans. However, the ELAS had become heroes by capturing the Germans and were building up their reputation. They wanted more Greeks to join them in the battle against the Germans. According to some reports, the ELAS were actually hoping for a bloody response from the Germans that would rally the local Greeks to join their ranks.

The prisoners were kept in a large building in Mazeika guarded by no more than seven Andartes. Their leader was the former artillery captain of the Greek army, Sotirios Theodorakopoulos, a man of about 35 years old, who came from the village of Arbounas at Kalavryta. During their captivity the Germans were made to perform hard physical labor by the Andartes. Not all of

Captured German soldiers performing hard physical labor.

the prisoners did hard labor. The non-German prisoners in the group, such as the Alsatians, were treated much better than the Germans.

One non-German prisoner worked in the hairdressing salon, another for the village joiner (master craftsman), and a third at the tailors. The Germans were to stay in Mazeika for nearly seven weeks—enough time to create bonds between the villagers, the guards and the prisoners. The biggest problem was the care of the prisoners. Every day, the starving villagers had to provide the food rations for the 78 men and their Andartes guards.

For a time during November 1943, the German army leaders in the Peloponnese were talking through intermediaries with the Greek Andartes leaders, primarily a Greek priest named Chronis. They were negotiating for the release of the German soldiers being held as prisoners. In late October and early November, the Germans had been going all around the Peloponnese and taking hundreds of Greeks, perhaps as many as 4000, suspected of being Andartes or communists, as prisoners. Most were sent to concentration camps either in Athens or farther away, such as at Dachau. These negotiations did not go well; the Greeks kept asking for more and more in return for releasing their German prisoners. They ended up asking for 50 Greeks to be released for each German they would release. Also, they had requested specific individuals whom they especially wanted to be released. The Germans got tired of the constantly increasing demands. Eventually the negotiator was told to stop trying and that no exchange of prisoners would be agreed to. He then warned the Greeks in Kalavryta that there would be reprisals from the

Germans for not releasing the prisoners. Of course, even he did not know how bad those "atonement measures" would be.

In October or November of 1943, the Germans had come to the realization that they had little or no control over the mountainous areas of the Peloponnese, especially the Kalavryta region. Walter Barth, a German leader, said that the EAM (National Liberation Front) and ELAS had formed one state in the state and would exercise their communist governance unlimited. The mountainous interior is thus "completely under the rule of the gangs."[21]

This photo of the German prisoners and their guards was taken on October 28, 1943, in Priolithos, near Mazeika. On the right-hand side of the picture is barely decipherable writing, which roughly reads: "This is the proof that the invincible German fascists have been captured by the heroic ELAS. Priolithos, 28.10.1943."

---

[21] Meyer, *From Vienna to Kalavryta* (translated from the German by Theodore P. Georgas).

"Operation Kalavryta" in 1943

The following account of "Operation Kalavryta" is from Hermann Frank Meyer's *From Vienna to Kalavryta* (interpreted from the German by Theodore P. Georgas):[22]

> German general Karl von Le Suire appointed Willibald Akamphuber (SS execution squad) leader of the "Operation Kalavryta" company.
>
> Akamphuber had been jointly responsible, with the 749th Regiment, for the horrific massacres of the Serb population in Kragujevac and Kraljevo in October 1941. Garhöfer recalls that Akamphuber was called by his comrades "Al Capone," after the notorious Chicago felon and mafia leader. Obviously impressed by the "reliable and experienced leader," Le Suire also made Akamphuber responsible in September for the new convict train. Le Suire saw in this "Al Capone" all the qualities he felt necessary to lead such a move: "Toughness, recklessness, male discipline, and unconditional command obedience."
>
> The German leaders knew their efforts to stop the Andartes were useless. Raids on German truck columns, railway security and smaller squads would now happen almost daily. German companies' ongoing operations would largely be failures, as the gangs' tactics were to avoid major hostilities with German troops. On the basis of

---

[22] Meyer, *From Vienna to Kalavryta* (translated from the German by Theodore P. Georgas).

enemy reports, Le Suire was informed that the gangs' centers were in the area of Kalavryta, Mazeika, Mira and Koumari. In the past two weeks alone there had been more than 20 incidents against German troops in this area.

The strength of the Andartes groups in Kalavryta, Mazeika, Mira and Koumari was estimated by the V-men (undercover Gestapo agents) to be 300. They would appear in groups of only 60–100 men, but they were constantly on the move, and with the exception of Kalavryta and Mira (villages that were considered to be constantly occupied by Andartes), they would only occasionally be forced into the villages. Their armament was called "very good"—in addition to rifles and hand grenades, they were equipped with heavy and light machine guns and submachine guns. Their clothing "consisted largely of civilian clothes mixed with individual uniform pieces of Greek and Italian origin," and the footwear was very poor.

Major Walter Barth, who was the General Staff Officer for leadership and tactics had reported to General La Suire that the situation had dramatically worsened, from a German point of view. One day later, two additional messages arrived, which led Le Suire to drastically change course. He decided that the Akamphuber combat group would execute hostages as atonement for the killed German soldiers.

The first incident was a raid on a German car, which was committed on November 23rd at Nikoleika on the highway between Patras and Corinth. In the process, a lieutenant named Röver was killed, Lieutenant Count von Bothmer wounded, and the driver of the car taken away. And in the second case, "about 50 partisans from positions on either side of the road" between Sparta and Gytheio raided a German truck crew. After the Germans sent a "relief column" to the scene, "the partisans fled into the mountains" so that they could not be made to fight. In this attack, the Germans had 4 dead, 10 seriously wounded and 12 lightly wounded.

On November 24, Le Suire responded to these attacks by ordering the shooting of 20 communist leaders as a provisional atonement measure for killing Lieutenant Röver. At the same time, the 1st Battalion of the 737th Regiment carried out a search operation in Sparta, in which three Greeks, rifles, pistols, ammunition, and propaganda material were captured.

Then, on November 25, between Sparta and Tripoli, another German truck crew was attacked by partisans. This time four Germans were killed and nine went missing (they never returned to their unit). In reprisal, Le Suire ordered the immediate execution of 100 hostages at the scene of the attack. Presumably, the deaths of the four Germans who were killed on November 23 during the raid on the truck column between Sparta and Gytheio were also being atoned for. Although the war diary entry of November 26 stated that "as a provisional measure of atonement for the gang robbery on the Tripoli–Sparta road at the raiding point [Monodendri], 100 hostages from the Tripoli camp" were shot dead, but the number of victims is incorrect.

On the way to the execution site, in a rage over the murder of their comrades, the Germans took '18 farmers and shepherds in the fields and executed them, together with the 100 hostages". Thus, a total of 118 Greeks were killed. The name of one of the victims, the doctor Karvounis, has been unforgotten until today. Although the Germans wanted to spare him, the doctor insisted on, as eyewitnesses remember, being shot with his compatriots.

ΚΟΙΝΟΠΟΙΗΣΙΣ

Ώς ἐξελεαστικὸν μέτρον διὰ τὴν δειλὴν καὶ ἐπίβουλον ἐπίθεσιν ἀνταρτῶν εἰς γερμανικὴν φάλαγγα αὐτοκινήτων εἰς τὸν δρόμον Τριπόλεως Σπάρτης τὴν ἡμέραν 25 Νοεμβρίου 1943 ἐξετελέσθησαν οἱ κάτωθι:

ΤΗΝ 26 ΝΟΕΜΒΡΙΟΥ ΕΙΣ ΤΟΠΟΝ ΕΦΟΡΜΗΣΕΩΣ

1) Φράγγος Προκόπιος   ἐκ Τριπόλεως
2) Χαρίτος Ἀθανάσιος   »
3) Σαρδέλλης Νικόλαος   »
4) Χρονόπουλος Σωτήριος   »
5) Χρυσοβιτσιώτης Ἀθανάσιος   »
6) Κορωνιὸς Γεώργιος   »
7) Παπαπλίου Χρῖστος   ,
8) Γιατράκος Γεώργιος   ἐκ Σπάρτης
9) Ἀνδριτσάκης Παναγιώτης
10) Τριήρης Λεωνίδας
11) Ἀνδριτσάκης Σαράντος
12) Ἀλεμαγκίδης Δημήτριος
13) Κοκκιμέλης Νικόλαος
14) Τζιβανόπουλος Ἰωάννης
15) Τζιβανόπουλος Δημοσθένης
16) Παπαδάκος Γρηγόριος
17) Λυώνιας Δημήτριος
18) Κουτσονικόλης Εὐθύμιος
19) Μακρῆς Γεώργιος
20) Ἀλεμαγκίδης Ζαχαρίας
21) Ἀλεμαγκίδης Ἰωάννης
22) Κόντος Θεόδωρος
23) Χίας Θεόδωρος
24) Βουλόκκος Πέτρος
25) Κουτονμιάτος Τζανέτος
26) Καραγιαννάκος Ἰωάννης
27) Ἀντωνόπουλος Γεώργιος
28) Τζιβανόπουλος Παρασκευᾶς
29) Τζιβανόπουλος Σωκράτης
30) Κεχαγιᾶς Εὐάγγελος
31) Κεχαγιᾶς Ἠλίας
32) Κεχαγιᾶς Νικόλαος
33) Μαμινάκη Βασιλική
34) Φικιώρης Μελέτιος
35) Καρβούνης Χρῖστος
36) Ζερβομιχάλος Ἀντώνιος
37) Σάλμης Ἠλίας
38) Γκοιζώλης Γεώργιος
39) Θεοφύλης Ἀνάργυρος
40) Κοντάκος Ἠλίας
41) Λαμπρόπουλος Σπύρος
42) Ντιαριώτης Παναγιώτης
43) Καφεντζόπουλος Κων)νος
44) Φλώρος Ἰωάννης
45) Ράπατας Κων)νος
46) Κουτρουμάνης Παναγιώτης
47) Τριήρης Ἀντώνιος
48) Λιμπεϊζιώνης Νικόλαος
49) Ἀλιμήσης Σπύρος
50) Κιρκινέζος Ἰωάννης
51) Μανωλόπουλος Ἐμμανουήλ.
52) Γιαννακόπουλος Παναγιώτης
53) Καρτερούλης Δημήτριος
54) Τζιτζέρης Νικόλαος
55) Αὔγχρης Νικόλαος
56) Βωξίλας Γεώργιος
57) Σηροδινὸς Γεώργιος
58) Σηροδινὴς Νικόλαος
59) Στελάκης Παναγιώτης
60) Σηροδινὸς Ἀνδρέας
61) Θεοφυλογιαννάκος Γεώργιος
62) Μανιάτης Στάθρος
63) Παπαδόγιαννης Νικόλαος
64) Δραγκάρης Σπῦρος
65) Κουρνιώτης Νικόλαος
66) Χατζιπετράκος Ἰωάννης
67) Μπλάθρας Παναγιώτης
68) Μπλάθρας Γεώργιος
69) Τζίγκος Κων)νος
70) Ζωφρόπουλος Χαράλαμπος
71) Παπαστάθης Νικόλαος
72) Παπαστάθης Εὐάγγελος
73) Στευράκος Ὀθόνιμος
74) Στευράκος Δημήτριος
75) Φιλιππόπουλης Παναγιώτης
76) Εὐσταθιάδης Ἀναστάσιος
77) Θεοδωρόπουλος Ἀνάργυρος
78) Ζερβούλιας Σταμάτιος
79) Κυριαζῆς Ἠλίας
80) Κόσιβας Παρασκευᾶς
81) Κεφαλᾶς Χαρίλαος
82) Τσελέκης Ἰωάννης
83) Πέρμπας Λυμπέρης
84) Ρουμελιώτης Παναγιώτης   Μαγούλα
85) Κοντογιάνος Λυμπέρης
86) Κωνστάντης Βασίλειος
87) Ἀλεβετσιωβίτης Μιχαήλ
88) Σοριάνης Κωσμᾶς
89) Γεωργόπουλος Ἰωάννης
90) Μαχφιλιᾶς Γεώργιος   Μυστρᾶ
91) Καρβούνης Κωνσταντίνος   Σκούρα
92) Παπακωνσταντίνος Ἀθαν.   Ἀνώγεια
93) Πλάγος Γεώργιος   »
94) Κονφῆς Σπύρος   »
95) Καραχάλιος Σπύρος   Βαμβακού
96) Χατζιπετράκος Παναγιώτης   Παρόρι
97) Μιχαλόπουλος Χρῆστος   »
98) Μητράκος Ἀπόστολος   Πλάτανα
99) Μενεγάκος Ἐμμανουήλ.   Γύθειον
100) Σπιφάκος Κυριάκος   »

Ο ΣΤΡΑΤΙΩΤΙΚΟΣ ΔΙΟΙΚΗΤΗΣ ΠΕΛΟΠΟΝΝΗΣΟΥ

*Notice posted by the Germans: As an exploratory measure for the timid and pernicious attack on a German automobile on the road from Tripoli to Sparta on November 25, 1943, the following were held. **And then executed**. Source: Meyer, From Vienna to Kalavryta.*

38

The ELAS/Andartes were led by Dimitrios Michos, who had his headquarters 2.5 miles (4 km) west of Kalavryta in the small village of Vissoka.

Vissoka, Vissotia, Visoka—now known as Skepasto—is a very lovely village, with impressive town planning. It's 4 km west of Kalavryta and opposite Agia Lavra Monastery. The history of the village goes back to the 15th century. Before the war, the village enjoyed considerable economic development. However, it was bombed by the German forces on November 29, 1943, killing 13 residents. On December 14, 1943, after the Kalavryta holocaust on the 13th, the village was set on fire by the Germans.[23]

These events led to the total breakdown of negotiations for the release of the captured 78 German soldiers.

The day after the 118 Greeks were executed, all efforts to peacefully end the problem of the prisoners came to an end. Michos sent Le Suire a last plea to release the Greeks held in prison camps in exchange for the German prisoners.

Le Suire answered Michos' last note with violence by ordering the bombing of the suspected ELAS headquarters. Twelve Stukas of the X. Fliegerkorps (planes of the 10th flight squadron) flew to attack the village of Skepasto (Vissoka) on November 29 and landed a direct hit on the elementary school, in the immediate vicinity of the Andartes leader, who had stayed with his staff. However, at the time of the bombing he was not there. Several houses of the village went up in flames. The teacher was able to rescue the children, but 13 villagers lost their lives.

---

[23] Skepasto, https://www.exploring-greece.gr/en/show/42099/:ttd/SKEPASTO#.XFRwAlVKi70

On December 13, 1999, the former mayor of Skepasto handed
Hermann F. Meyer a list of the names of the dead:

1. Nikolaos Karamousis
2. Georgios Antonakopoulos
3. Dimitrios Antonakopoulos
4. Athanasios Gidas
5. Akrivoula Katsikopoulou
6. Anathasios Danos
7. Panagiotis Andriopoulos
8. Athanasios Bourogiannis
9. Anastasios Papafraggos
10. Stathoula Andrikopoulou
11. Panagiotis Petroutsos
12. Christos Deodorakopoulos
13. Nikolaos Kanellis

The last three on the list came from Doumena and were
probably in Skepasto by chance; and Stathoula Andrikopoulou
came from Priolithos.[24]

None of the victims were known to be part of ELAS/Andartes.
This is because when the Andartes heard that Germans might
bomb their headquarters they fled Vissoka and hid up in the
mountains. When the 12 planes of the 10th flight squadron were
headed for Vissoka, more than 100 children were in the school.
The planes flew over and dropped the deadly bombs all over the
village. The teacher, Leonidas Charalambopoulos, acted quickly.
He heroically saved the children, keeping them inside the
building during the first pass of the planes, and then getting

---

[24] Meyer, *From Vienna to Kalavryta* (translated from the German by Theodore P.
Georgas).

them out of the school building before the bombers returned for their second raid. On the second bombing pass the Germans destroyed the school, which they had targeted as the ELAS/Andartes headquarters.[25]

On December 4, 1943, Le Suire issued the order to create a company codenamed "Kalawrita," which consisted of the bulk of the division. The company was given the goal of destroying deadly gangs in the area of Patras, Mazeika, Kalavryta and Tripia.

The Germans finally got the idea to bring in troops from all around the Peloponnese and even other parts of Greece to try to capture these rebels that were causing them so much trouble. In addition, they were trying to find the missing Schober combat group of 81 men. They decided to come at the Kalavryta area from three directions with three larger companies. The troops came from Tripoli, Aigio and Patras (that is, the south, north and northwest) simultaneously. The east was thought unnecessary, since the high mountains were not easily traversed, especially with winter weather starting. Their instructions were as follows:

> The success of the company is not based on terrain gain but on the extent of enemy losses and the spoils. It is important to find the gangs in their hiding place, to fight and shoot the men, and to burn down their villages. In the gang area it must be expected that the population will have a hostile attitude. Particular attention should be paid to all monasteries, chapels and isolated houses, as there are usually hidden weapons in storage that can be

---

[25] Popis Katsirodis, speech at the Memorial Event in Skepasto, November 27, 2017. http://www.kalavrytanet.com/arthro/e-omilia-tes-dikegoroy-popes-katsirode-sten-ekdelose-mnemes-sto-skepasto

expected. When German troops are entering a village, any civilian traffic from place to place is immediately to be prevented, as well as the ringing of church bells. All suspected inhabitants, men and women, are to be taken hostage.[26]

Besides the Germans stepping up pressure on the Kalavryta region, the Greek Andartes also stepped up their efforts, becoming stronger in numbers.

In September 1943, after the withdrawal of the Italians troops, the leaders of the ELAS in the Peloponnese decided to get organized so that they could negotiate with the British as one voice. The Peloponnesian ELAS, which was called the 8th Battalion, already had a command structure on the Greek mainland, where the ELAS troops were led by Aris Velouchiotis (kapetanios, i.e., captain), Stefanos Sarafis (στρατιωτικοσ, i.e., commander-in-chief) and Andreas Tzimas (politikos, i.e., politician). In the Peloponnese, Dimitrios Michos was considered the commander of the ELAS 8th Battalion. He was assisted by Pantelis Laskas (nom de guerre [assumed name] Pelopidas) as kapetanios and Nikos Thienis (nom de guerre Papoua) and Yiannis Michalopoulos (nom de guerre Orion) as politikos.[27]

Practically every day the Greeks were attacking the Germans all around the northern Peloponnese and making their lives miserable. They captured two larger groups of German on two occasions; they frequently shot and killed and wounded several

---

[26] Meyer, *From Vienna to Kalavryta* (translated from the German by Theodore P. Georgas).

[27] Meyer, *From Vienna to Kalavryta* (translated from the German by Theodore P. Georgas).

German soldiers. The German leadership was getting tired of the whole situation and was feeling pressure to get the area under firm control. But instead of gaining control they felt they were losing control to the ELAS/Andartes.

But this ELAS command structure did not last long. With the intention of ushering in the final phase of the Resistance struggle, the first Pan-Peloponnesian Congress of Resistance Organizations was held on November the 28th and 30th. All the key representatives of the local EAM, ELAS, EPON and EA organizations were there. On the initiative of the Athens EAM leadership, the participants decided on the military and political leadership of the Peloponnesian ELAS.

Since Yiannis Michalopoulos, alias Orion, had been sent to southern Messenia in October to build up the Resistance movement, a new leadership group had to be elected: Dimitrios Michos was appointed division kapetanios, while Dimitrios Kassandras (aka Alexandros), who had just arrived on the peninsula, was appointed commander by Michos. At the same time, Polydoros Daniilidis (aka Achilleas) was promoted to politikos.

All units of the ELAS were modeled after the former Greek army in the Third Peloponnesian Division. The division was divided into tagmata (battalions) and syntagmata (regiments). In all, the 6th Corinthian, the 8th Laconic, the 9th Messenian, the 11th Arcadian, the 12th Archean-elite Regiment, and the independent battalions of Kalavryta and Agialia were formed. The importance attached by the Central Committee of the ELAS to the newly structured Peloponnesian ELAS can be seen from the fact that it received its general instructions directly from Athens.

The strength of the regiments is contradictory. According to German knowledge, the Third Division alone in the Patras–Kalavryta–Aigio area consisted of about 1500–2000 combat troops, based on 1500–2000 men as a reserve. Usually the so-called ELAS reserve consisted of farmers, who, according to the Germans, performed their fieldwork peacefully during the day and attacked German posts at night. In total, these farmers had about 200 machine guns and pistols, 5000 rifles, 200 pistols, hand grenades, 4–8 grenade launchers, and English radios.

The German defense knew about the activities of the Andartes in other provinces of the Peloponnese, such as Laconia, Messinia and Arcadia. However, it had not been attacked in these regions to the same extent as in the north. The Germans merely suspected that there were "about 3000 well-armed bandits" who could fall back on a "reserve" of about 2500 men if necessary.[28]

---

[28] Meyer, *From Vienna to Kalavryta* (translated from the German by Theodore P. Georgas).

Battle of Pangrati[29] on December 5, 1943

On December 4, 1943, at 1 pm a German combat group under Captain Gnass set out on its return to Vytina. It arrived at about 4 pm and was reinforced with the 11th and 13th companies of the 737th Regiment, a mountain battery (3rd Artillery Regiment 670), an engineer platoon and a medical convoy. These additional troops, led by 31-year-old Captain Karl Kockert, were gathered in Megalopolis on December 2nd and marched from there with their pack animals via Moulatsi and Dimitsana to Vytina in two days. On the morning of December 5th, the troops moved out together to fulfill their mission of securing the area northwest of Mazeika and preventing the enemy from escaping south. Because of the different kinds of equipment, supplies, vehicles and pack animals they had, the combat groups were divided into a mountain mobile unit, with the animals, under the leadership of Kockert, and a motorized, or street, mobile unit under Gnass.

After the departure, the Kockert group searched the villages of Granitsa, now known as Nymfasia, and Kamenitsa, from which the population had not fled. According to an interrogation, the residents said that the Andartes leader Christos Stassinopoulos had stayed there on December 3rd and then marched on to his seat at Dara. As Kockert proceeded farther north of the village of Dara, he opened fire on the fleeing civilians because he suspected them to be gang members. He also arrested seven Greeks doing fieldwork, whom he committed to repairing the roads and bridges that had been blown up in many places.

---

[29] Referred to as Pagkrati by Hermann Frank Meyer.

Meanwhile, the Gnass motorized group had reached Pangrati, which lies between Mazeika and Dara. Here Gnass was bombarded on the half slope near the village around 1:15 pm by machine gun and rifle fire from favorable mountain positions. Kockert heard this message over the radio, so he left Dara to relieve Gnass's units. It was not until the Germans made it to the heights in a swift attack, according to Gnass's report, that the bandits stopped firing, and about 100–150 men fled northward. In

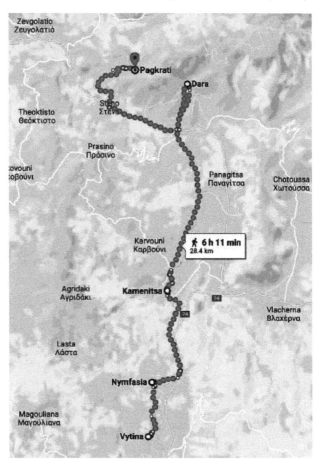

Route taken by Kockert from Vytina to Pangrati.
Map created using google Maps.

this battle, the Germans had to mourn one dead and one lightly wounded, while they counted eight dead Andartes on the battlefield.

After the altercation, both of the German combat groups occupied Pangrati. The village was searched, and the inhabitants

46

were questioned. The pastor of the village said that 22 Russians (aka communists), who had fled the Germans from Tripoli together with 80 Greeks under the leadership of the former captain of the Greek army, Christos Stassinopoulos, had occupied Pangrati on the evening of December 3rd, plundered the population, and stayed at the school.

The Russians, armed with eight German machine guns, had fired during the attack on the Germans, while the Greek partisans had retreated to the rear mountain positions. The Russians were dressed in German uniforms. On their caps was the inscription ELAS with a Soviet star attached. The Greeks, on the other hand, wore civilian clothes and various captured uniform pieces.

In all likelihood these men were not Russians but Turkmen that had defected to the ELAS, serving in the Turkmen Battalion of the 117th Jäger (aka Hunters) Division, like many Italians, as committed volunteers (aka Hiwis). These men were armed and dressed in German uniforms and were used primarily for protection and security tasks, as well as for the expansion of current positions. Since there had been numerous overflows to the gangs, Le Suire had asked his commanders, after resumption of his service, about the Turkmen immorally and willfully aiding the enemy. To prevent a further occurrence, Le Suire adopted strict rules. These rules were that the Turkmen had to deliver their weapons after service and were not allowed to be on the street or in a restaurant. They were monitored day and night and had to stay in separate quarters after the 8:00 pm curfew. Le Suire had forbidden them, as he put it, to "reside in the rooms of my soldiers."

The pastor of Pangrati told the Germans that the Andartes had known since December 3rd that the Germans were marching from the direction of Aigio to Kalavryta with 500 mules. They knew that the German intention was to surround the Andartes and Kalavryta from all sides. Consequently, the Andartes had already withdrawn from the area.

According to these statements, as punishment for the capture of the German soldiers, Pangrati was burnt down and the male population was shot dead. It appears that Kockert intended to comply with Le Suire's order that places be burned down and the men shot. In fact, although Pangrati was destroyed, the male population of the village was not shot dead.

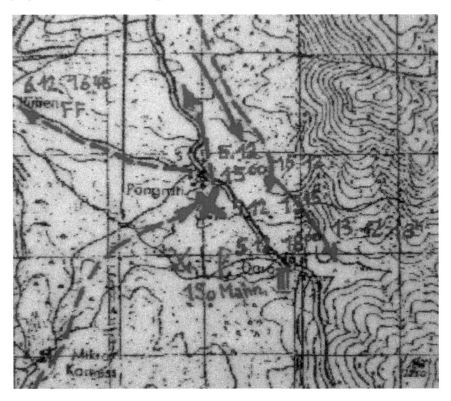

German record of troop movements and destruction of Pagrati on December 5, 1943.
Source: Courtesy of the Municipal Museum of the Kalavrytan Holocaust.

The contemporary witness Maria Korbis, who was then 16 years old, reported, "Most of the houses had already been destroyed by the Italians in July 1943. The Germans burned only a few houses down but drove off our herds—and our men. In the evening, seven farmers from Dara were shot dead in Pangrati in retaliation for a killed German soldier."[30] The unfortunate victims were the peasants whom Kockert had picked up during fieldwork and had committed to road and bridge repair.

The huts were for the most part simple dwellings and sheepfolds, which were used by shepherds only in the summer. Andartes always used a hut as a welcome shelter. To destroy these settlements, Kockert went with his troops on December 7th west of the main road via Filia and Tsorota before Mazeika, where he was to search the monastery Athanasios. Since the engineers had not yet succeeded in restoring the bridge over the Aroanios, which had been blown up by the Andartes on December 6th, the crossing of the river and the subsequent ascent to the monastery were extremely laborious.

Finally, the monastery was completely burned out, and a little later, the neighboring village of Filia was found half destroyed. Here the inhabitants came to the soldiers with raised arms and reported that the destruction had been carried out during the Italian occupation.[31]

---

[30] Meyer, *From Vienna to Kalavryta* (translated from the German by Theodore P. Georgas).
[31] Meyer, *From Vienna to Kalavryta* (translated from the German by Theodore P. Georgas).

Residents of Pangrati (and other villages) were forced to rebuild the bridge over the Aroanios River.

In the course of this day, it was engineers, a cyclist squadron, and according to several German reports, volunteers from the population who finally managed to make the bridge over the Aroanios usable again. They also repaired the main road to Mazeika, which had been made unusable by numerous obstructions and explosions. So Gnass, with his motorized reconnaissance unit, reached Mazeika around 4 pm, the same time as Kockert, who was marching with his mountain mobile group, arrived.[32]

By December 9, 1943, the German army had grown significantly and started to close in from all sides of the Kalavryta region:

> Thus, the original Kalawrita company had become a major corporation, employing more than 3000 soldiers from all North Peloponnese stations, Tripoli, Patras, Aigio, Corinth and Pyrgos, in a concentric company with the objective of being in the area to encircle and destroy Kalavryta's supposed enemy.[33]

---

[32] Meyer, *From Vienna to Kalavryta* (translated from the German by Theodore P. Georgas).
[33] Ibidem.

Holocaust of Kalavryta, December 1943

The German army would hit Kalavryta hard with reprisals under the code name of "Operation Kalavryta." The Germans came into Kalavryta on Thursday, December 9, 1943. They created a stranglehold around the city so no one could escape. As the residents were deeply concerned, they appealed to the German commander, who assured them that no one would suffer anything and that their goal was the extermination of only the rebels. Initially they proceeded to set fire to houses belonging to guerrillas and sought revenge for German casualties of the Battle of Kerpini.

On Sunday, December 12th, the Germans began making preparations to leave the next day. The villagers were happy that the Germans were apparently leaving, but they were also wary of how badly hurt the Germans would leave the village. On the morning on Monday, December 13th, before dawn, the Germans rang the bells of the main church. The German officers and soldiers ordered the people to gather all residents at the elementary school and told them that they should bring along a blanket and enough food for a day. Once the residents arrived at the school building, the Germans sorted them by sex and age and separated the families. The women were barricaded in the school. Men 13 years of age and older were driven in groups to the nearby slope on the ridge of Kappi. The Germans had carefully selected this site. The slope was like an amphitheater and would not allow anyone to escape. The people of Kalavryta were then forced to see their properties, homes and entire city burned to the ground. None of the residents knew what was planned for them. Besides all of their possessions, they themselves were to be burned to death, all of the women and children trapped in the school building, guarded by fully armed soldiers.

Greek Andartes near Kalavryta August 1944.
Source: Meyer, From Vienna to Kalavryta.

The Germans had stripped the town of all valuables, livestock and crops. Homes, shops and warehouses were all stripped bare. The Germans collected the money and stocks in the banks and any public buildings, after forcing the managers to deliver the valuables.

Then, from the Alexander the Great hotel the Germans sent up a green flare, and then a red one, which was the sign to begin the execution. **On the slope of Kappi, machine guns mowed down the men of Kalavryta.** After the shooting had ceased, only 13 men survived. That anyone survived was a miracle, as after the initial shooting the Germans went through all the bodies so they could finish off anyone that wasn't dead. They shot each man and boy gathered there in the head with a killing shot at point blank range. One man miraculously survived after being shot directly in the forehead. A few others were just grazed by the kill shot. Nearly 700 men and boys were executed.

In the elementary school, the women and children experienced moments of confusion. At first, they smelled smoke and heard the sounds of the entire village being set on fire. The Germans went door to door and lit every building.

The Kalavrytans realized in their horror that the school they were locked in was also on fire. The windows were barred over and high up, so getting out through them was problematic. They managed to smash through the windows and bars enough so they could drop their children out. Many children suffered broken legs and other injuries from the fall. Finally, some women got the front door of the building open and were able to escape the fire. Either the Germans had decided to leave the entrance unguarded or they didn't have the heart to let the captives all die in the burning building.

The women tried to find their family members in the mass confusion. The village was so smoke filled that no one could see anything. Even though it was the middle of a sunny afternoon, the sky was as black as the darkest night. People went to see if anything was left of their homes. However, very few homes survived the fires.

Initially, the women thought that the men and boys had been taken prisoner and removed from the village, but then they saw groups of German soldiers coming back from the hill of Kappi. The Germans were singing a happy song that was a hit tune of that year, as if they were so happy with their lives.

Then one by one and in small groups the women heard that the men and older boys had been killed. So the women started to ascend the hill to the place where the German soldiers had led the men. They found the most horrific and inhumane spectacle—men, boys, fathers, sons and brothers lying dead in a river of blood.

Statue at the Municipal Museum of the Kalavrytan Holocaust of a woman dragging her dead husband to the cemetery while her children watch.

The great massacre of Kalavryta was over, but the suffering was just beginning. The youth, the creative forces of the city, the fortunes and the years of laboring to build the town were all wiped out at 2:34 pm on December 13, 1943, as shown by the hands of the stopped church clock.

The drama continued as the surviving women struggled with their bare hands to dig makeshift graves in the frozen December earth to bury their dead. They used their blankets to drag the killed men, teenaged boys, women and children to the cemetery.

In the Place of Execution, there now stands a huge white cross and petrified mother statue, eternal symbols of martyrdom. This is meant to send messages of peace and brotherhood to people of the world.

Others were buried there on the hill where they had fallen, a tragic scene that lasted for days. Then the survivors had to find a way to survive in the rubble of the town that had been built to house families for years to come, all destroyed in a day. Only 8 houses out of nearly 500 were left standing.

The Holocaust of Kalavryta had a huge effect that the Germans had not anticipated. It touched the hearts and minds of all Greeks and united them. It greatly strengthened their will to fight against the foreign occupiers. The women of Kalavryta, the Kalavryta mothers, heroically fought difficult conditions and managed to raise their children and rebuild the town from the ruins. [34]

The occupation by the Italians and German armies was a most difficult and stirring period of modern Greek history. The Greeks had to face multiple hardships: invading conquerors, the problem of survival, the pain of starvation, executions, torture and destruction. The area in and around Kalavryta, an area with a long history and revolutionary past, suffered like no others in all of Greece. There were enormous losses of the workforce, with mass executions of civilians and outright disasters.

---

[34] Official website of the Municipality of Kalavryta
http://www.kalavrita.gr/information/istoria/item/809-to-olokaytoma-ton-kalavryton

According to German Army reports, in the summer of 1943, the Germans began executions, bombardment and destruction of villages. The list of events that destroyed villages is rather lengthy. I won't list all of the German atrocities here, but the report filed by the commander at the end of the actions known as "Operation Kalavryta" sums up the damages:

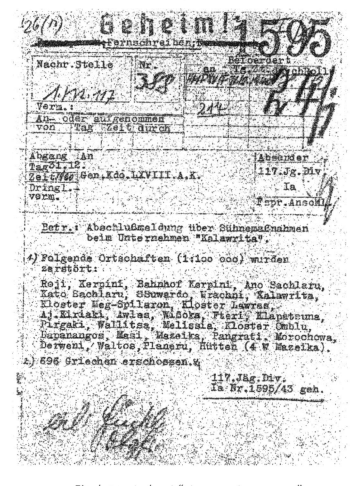

Final report about "atonement measures"
during "Operation Kalavryta."
Source: Municipal Museum of the Kalavritan Holocaust.

Στο απόρρητο ραδιογράφημα της 117 Jäger Division (Αρ.1595/43), καταγράφεται ο τελικός απολογισμός της Επιχείρησης Καλάβρυτα.

"(1) Κατεστράφησαν ολοκληρωτικά τα χωριά: Ρογοί, Κερπινή, Στάση Κερπινής, Άνω Ζαχλωρού, Κάτω Ζαχλωρού, Σούβαρδο, Βραχνί, Καλάβρυτα, Μοναστήρια Μεγάλου Σπηλαίου και Αγίας Λαύρας, Αγία Κυριακή, Αυλές, Βυσωκά, Φτέρη, Πλατανιώτισσα, Πυργάκι, Βάλτσα, Μελίσσια, Μοναστήρι Ομπλού, Λαπαναγοί, Μάζι, Μαζέικα, **Παγκράτι**, Μορόχωβα, Δερβένι, Βάλτος, Πλανητέρου, Καλύβια. (2) **696 Έλληνες εκτελέστηκαν....**" [35]

Translated, this report reads as follows:

In a secret radiogram, 117 Jäger Division (Ar.1595/43) recorded the final report of Operation Kalavryta:

"(1) Completely destroyed villages: Rogoi, Kerpini, near Kerpini, Ano Zachlorou, Kato Zachlorou, Souvardo, Vrachni, Kalavryta, Monastery of the Great Cave (Mega Spilaio), Monastery of Agia Lavra, Agia Kyriaki, Avles, Vysoka, Pteri, Plataniotissa, Pyrgaki, Valcea, Melissia, Monastery Omblos, Lapanagoi, Mazi, Mazeika (Kleitoria), **Pangrati**, Morochova, Derveni, Valtos, Planitero Kalyvia. (2) **696 Greeks executed....**"

---

[35] Meyer, *From Vienna to Kalavryta, page 324*

More than 600 died at Kalavryta on December 13th. Survivors stated that when the Germans machine-gunned the crowd, they had been covered by the dead when they fell. The women and children managed to free themselves from the flaming school while the rest of the town was set ablaze. The following day the Nazi troops burned down the Agia Lavra monastery, a landmark of the Greek War of Independence.

In total, nearly 700 civilians (the actual number is probably over 1500) were reportedly killed during the reprisals of Operation Kalavryta. For instance, my great-grandmother is not on any list of people who died at the hands of the Nazis at this time, but we know she died in the house fires. Twenty-eight communities—towns, villages, monasteries and settlements—were destroyed. In the region in and around Kalavryta about 1000 houses were looted and burned, and more than 2000 farm animals were seized by the Germans. These large numbers are not confirmed and maybe exaggerations. The Kalavryta officials after the war were known to use larger numbers such as 1000 were killed in the massacre on December 13th. No list of victims has ever been produced with 100 names on it. However, a look at the total deaths in the entire region around Kalavryta this 1000 number is closer to being true. The officials most likely increased their claims in order to secure more aid. Their village had been totally destryoed and the world powers, such as Britan and the USA were not providing much in the way of financial assistance to Kalavryta. They felt they were being ignored. This probably was not intentional but due to the fact that most of Europe and places all around the world had been destroyed or had horrible loss of life. There simply were not enough Red Cross workers or aid to fix every issue. It would be many years until Kalavryta got financial aid and then it was a small amount.

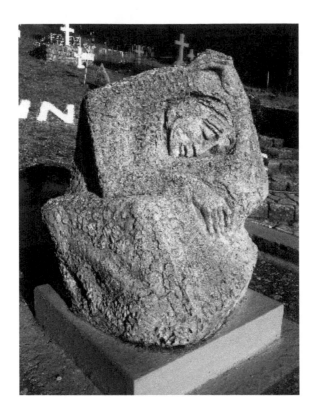

In the Place of Execution in Kalavryta, the petrified mother statue.

Before the massacre at Kalavryta the Germans were trying to get the local Greeks under control and stomp out the Resistance fighters. German soldiers came and went to Kalavryta, Mazeika and through the area of Pangrati to Tripoli, where the headquarters for the Italian army was located. Each time they would go back and forth from Kalavryta to Tripoli. Pangrati was located right in the middle and next to the two rivers, where they would stop to get water.

When the German forces passed through Pangrati, they would torture the key people, including the doctor and the priest, to find out where the Greek rebels were hiding and who in the village was plotting against them.

There was a priest in Pangrati, Panagiotis Charalambopoulos, who was tortured. His grandson wrote about it; he either witnessed it first-hand or heard the story passed down from villagers that had witnessed what happened. The German soldiers repeatedly tortured Panagiotis, but each time the priest gave up no information. He would only tell the Germans that they could do whatever they wanted to him and that he would gladly die for the Greek cause.

The German soldiers tried to hang Father Panagiotis three times. Each time they hanged him the rope broke, and the priest fell to the ground. He rose up, and the Germans were shocked that he was still alive. They hanged him again, and the same thing happened. The soldiers were astonished that the rope broke a second time and did not want to hang him again, but the commander insisted. So, they hanged him a third time. Each time they checked the rope to make sure it was sturdy. When the rope broke the third time, the German soldiers thought it must be divine intervention, so they refused orders to hang the priest a fourth time. They simply walked away. The commander found some other German soldiers nearby, whom he ordered to kill the priest. Those ones did not hang him, but instead killed him by stabbing him repeatedly with their bayonets. The priest never gave up any information, and he never lost his faith in God before they killed him.

Below are more details of the priest's torture and murder, which occurred in July of 1944, as told by his grandson, which I have interpreted from Greek. This account also tells of a second village priest, Argyris Soukas, who was also tortured and murdered at the hand of the German soldiers.

Touching Texts for Both National Martyrs, Memorable Priests of Our Village, Argyris Soukas and Panagiotis Charalambopoulos

This is the story of the sacrifice of two priests, Argyris Soukas and Panagiotis Charalambopoulos, who were martyred for our nation during the German army occupation. This story moves the public, and even all political factions.

It was not because it was the sacrifice of two people; it was a superhuman sacrifice that affected the whole nation and took shape and appeared with the holy soul and body of the two priests of our village. This testimony to the proud and heroic attitude of fortitude, even in the face of torture and death, did not remain a local event by any means. The entire world heard of the atrocities carried out against our people by the German army in the bloodstained land of Kalavryta.

This violence exceeded all limits and created a national voice that was heard across the length and breadth of our country. The radio, newspapers, magazines and publications of all kinds presented it as evidence from our great nation that had endured years of sacrifices. It is difficult to name and present all facts that very movingly reported the martyred sacrifice.

But we cannot stay indifferent to a large text, published for many years in the magazine *Treasure* by John B. Ioannidis, journalist, of the voluntary passion of our two priests that became known throughout Greece. [36]

---

[36] Φιλοποιμην Π. Βλαγκοπουλοσ, Το Παγκρατι, Μια μικρη περιληψη της ιστορικης του διαδρομης 1687–2007; Εκδοση Συλλογου Παγκρατιωτων Καλαβρυτινων, Ο Αγιοσ Ιωαννησ Ο Θεολογοσ, Αθηνα: 2008. [Filopoimin P. Vlangopoulos, *The Pangrati: A Brief Summary of the Historical Course 1687–2007*, Kalavryta Pangratian Association, Saint

This remarkable publication reported the event as follows:

> With the holy cross and rifle as my witness, the priest Argyris Soukas was an 80-year-old man when he was caught by the Germans. He was chaplain to the community Pangrati and the metropolitan region of Kalavryta.

Photo taken September 2018 of the bust of Priest Argyris Soukas, located in the square of Pangrati.

His whole life was a model of virtue. He was a real saint. And yet the beast Hitler did not respect either the robes that Soukas wore or his advanced

John the Theologist, Athens: 2008 (as translated from Greek by Theodore P. Georgas).]

age. Because in the area some strangers (Greek rebellion fighters) attacked a passing German phalanx, the German soldiers arrested 50 Greek hostages to execute.

Papa-Argyris then decided to visit the Germans to explain that those arrested had nothing to do with the attack. The conversation was as follows.

German soldier asked the priest, "And you, what are you? Their lawyer?"

The elder Argyris Soukas was not baffled. He responded through the interpreter. "No. The lads do not need a lawyer, because they are all innocent."

The German soldier pressed, "And how do you know that all of them are innocent? Who told you?"

Father Soukas answered, "There is no need for anyone to tell me. I have known all of them since birth. I baptized them, and I married them. So I can guarantee them with my own head."

The German laughed sarcastically and pushed. "Ok. I will leave, and others will keep you prisoner. Are you happy?"

The Father answered, "I am."

The priest showed unparalleled courage, knowing what the Germans would do to him. Because of their savagery, it was unthinkable that a priest would stand up to them.

They began to interrogate him and to ask him what relationship he had with the rebels. The interrogation lasted for hours. And because they did not manage to squeeze a word out of the priest, they submitted him to more torture. It was horrible to see the old man torn through the hands of the executioners at the time of the questioning.

The first thing the barbarians did was to uproot the beard from his face and then proceeded to pull out all his fingernails and toenails. Yet Father Argyris was smiling his biggest smile, as were the first martyrs of Christianity. It was July 20, 1944, and the heat was unbearable. Sweat trickled from his face; he was bleeding from the forehead as they slowly extinguished his eyes.

The German soldier then asked, "Are you going to talk now?"

Argyris Soukas replied, "I do not say anything."

The German soldier pressed on again. "You do not know or do not want to tell us."

Argyris Soukas boldly answered, "Whatever I know will not open up my mouth."

These responses further enraged the Germans. But they gave up on him for a bit, not because he regretted not speaking, but to rest themselves.

During this time, a known traitor made an appearance and affirmed that the priest had contact with the rebels and that he constantly spoke against Hitler. The Germans rolled the priest again in martyrdom.

Then the German soldier further questioned the priest, "Are you not sad that you will die? You are a very old man and should die quietly in your bed, not like this."

The elderly priest looked at him. "You can feel sorry for yourself," he told them. "For I do not care about your obsession with me. I will not tell you anything, nor curse you. Because thus I opened the road which leads straight toward the feet of God, while ye perish forever from the face of the earth."

The commanding officer then grabbed a bayonet and stabbed firmly into the chest of the venerable elder. Blood sprang from the wound. And yet the priest did not fall, nor make the slightest move in the face of death.

Then the brutal hand of the officer went down several times, each time sinking the bayonet into the priest. A torrent of expletives escaped from the profane and filthy mouth of the murderer. The voracious beast had awakened in him and could no longer be stopped. The German men looked satisfied. But a strange thing happened: Papa-Soukas, despite all the terrible wounds, was still alive and raised his brow. His eyes were alight; his lips, whispering prayers.

Father Soukas professed, "God, they do not know what they do. Forgive them."

Suddenly a young soldier drew his knife, grabbed the priest, put him on his knees, and sank the sharp metal into his neck. Blood sprang like a fountain and doused him.

But this blood caused the young German to become a demon. With a second blow, the head of the tragic priest almost detached from the trunk. The insides of Papa-Argyris fell on the bloodstained earth—torn open once, then two times and he remained motionless. He was dead.

The officer gestured to one of his men. He then thrust his lance with such momentum that the iron passed through the dead body and pinned the priest to the ground. Immediately some Germans began to dance around him. Others played, with a sense of accomplishment. They started photographing the dead priest and others to immortalize their awful feat.

But their rage did not stop there. Killing the priest with in such a terrible way was not enough. He still had to pay, even though he was lifeless. Without delay the soldiers were ordered to burn the house of the poor priest. Together they rushed to the spot, doused the house with gasoline, and set it on fire. The flames circled the foremost points. Fortunately, there was not anyone else there. The residents had managed to flee.

The turmoil lasted many hours. And when the simple accommodation of Father Argyris Soukas was nothing but ash, the Germans went on in a line and left singing.

Once the story of this evil deed became known, the population of the region rose up.

A local resident asked, "Will we just sit here with folded arms?"

Then another replied, "Will we let the beasts make us do what they want? No, it is better to have death than humiliation."

They were Greeks, one and all. For many decades the region had been making real young men. They never could tolerate slavery and always rebelled against each occupier. What could they do now, a handful of people, up against a relentless enemy, who had neither a holy God, nor a saint?

"We have to be patient, my children," said the new rector of the village, Panagiotis Charalambopoulos. "Only thus can we be vigilant. Otherwise you will make us all a mark."

"Let's toil," responded the most hot-blooded local Greek. "We will welcome them as suits them. The rifle our grandparents used will sing once again. As it was then, it will be now. Our ancestors started the revolution of 1821, and now we will start a new revolution."

But the prudent priest shook his head. "Let's not rush to our decisions. Today it is not enough to be a lad who only needs weapons to cope with them."

The angry man pushed, "And what do you suggest, Father?"

The holy leader answered, "I do not know yet. Let the current day pass, and tomorrow we will see what to do."

Panagiotis Charalambopoulos was a great clergyman, the most daring. He thought, "Let's grab the first rifle to avenge the unjust loss of my elder colleague, priest Argyris." But then he pondered the consequences. If he stood up to fight, his fellow citizens would of course follow him into battle, and this was not what he wanted. He risked getting them all killed if he started a revenge attack, and their deaths would be on his head.

In a battle, the Germans would leave none of them alive. Panagiotis Charalambopoulos had known the Germans well as he had observed them for about two years walking the Kalavryta region. Everywhere they passed the Germans left behind blood, tears and death.

"Isn't waiting until tomorrow too late?" they asked priest Panagiotis. "Do something to prepare for when the Germans return." They wanted to prevent him from leaving them in their time of need.

"You are right, my children. Those who wish to leave the village may hide in the caves. So if a battle is about to happen there will be no harm to you," said the priest.

"And you, what will be your fate, Father? Will you not come with us?" asked one of the local villagers.

"That can never be," he replied. "I will stay here. It is not right for all of us to leave our village deserted. Someone should be here when the Germans arrive. And that shall be me."

The villagers agreed, "Then we will not leave either. We shall stay here, and God help us." A few left the village, but the others did not want to show weakness. Such was their manliness.

As night fell and the people went to sleep, the terrible German beasts came out in the early morning. The Germans came to the home of Father Panagiotis and arrested him. They seemed hell-bent on apprehending all priests in the area.

As they had done with Father Argyris, they began to interrogate Father Panagiotis about things of which he had no idea. They set some wood on fire, but he did not find a word to say. The investigator, who knew that a beating would do nothing, ordered the Germans to cause him severe torment. They put skewers into his beard and twisted until it was half uprooted. They put an iron band around his head and slowly tightened it until blood come from his forehead.

The torturer threatened him. "Tell the truth to stop the pain. Otherwise you will die."

Father Panagiotis courageously responded, "A thousand times death, rather than be a betrayer."

The persecutor scolded him. "I pity your life?"

The good father said, "My life belongs to God and Fatherland."

The chief officer was the same one who had undone Father Soukas. He commanded his men to throw boiling oil on the priest's belly. Papa-Panagiotis closed his eyes and began to pray to occupy his thoughts, struggling without the consolation of even a single friend and without hope of receiving help from anyone. His resistance to torture resembled the patience of the saints.

No, he would not give them the satisfaction of seeing him bend. He clenched his teeth and was silent to the point that he actually sent the interrogator into despair. The bloodthirsty executioner instructed the interrogator to leave him alone for a little bit and maybe he would change his mind. They threw him into a basement. There, in the dark, the hapless priest let his soul be free. He wept and begged God to forgive him. The traitor interpreter heard this from outside. He ran to announce to the officer that they had broken the priest, exclaiming, "The priest is crying. Now he will say everything we want to hear."

The German commander listened desperately and shook his head. He said, "When a hero is crying, it means that he has decided to die. And since he is going to die, he will never speak."

This dialog was repeated by the interpreter himself in an apology that he wrote when he was captured by the Allies after his release in Italy.

Lying on the ground, the brave priest waited for the great moment. Whichever way he rested his body on the floor he was in terrible pain. Not even 10 minutes passed, and they took him upstairs again. New inquest, new torture.

The witness saw that the Germans could not make him talk, so they were commanded to hang him. The officer thought that with that command he would see the priest fall at his feet and beg for mercy. Instead, the clergyman raised his bloodied head and prepared to follow his executioners. He marched ahead of the officer so he would not delay his own execution.

The soldiers grabbed him, screaming. They tied a thick rope to the branch of a tree; they made a loop and passed it around his neck. The priest let the soldiers do what they wished. He did not show any resistance. He did not say a word.

"Will you confess?" the Germans asked.

The priest looked at the sky, smiled and closed his eyes. The Germans pulled the noose, but the rope broke, and the priest crashed to the ground. They cursed their religious enemies and prepared the gallows a second time. But again, the rope broke, as if God wanted to show them that they were committing a criminal act. However, instead of taming the beast, they only got angrier. They hanged him for a third time, and a third time it failed.

Most of the torturers took a few steps backward, fixated on the horror. They watched the priest Panagiotis in silence. The priest started smiling. It was something that nobody expected. What mysterious force could change the tragic destiny of the priest? Who cut the rope? Who else but God?

Nevertheless, the head officer, an atheist and pagan, gave a new command. "Take him immediately and complete the execution outside the village." Because the soldiers who attended the failed hanging hesitated to carry out the order, the officer sent other soldiers in their place.

Dragging the priest by the beard, they went through several narrow streets. Hitting him with their rifle butts, they forced him to proceed where they wanted. They arrived at a ditch, where they began new tortures. They cut off his beard, together with the skin, and then his hair. One soldier, who spoke a little Greek, asked him if he had anything to say.

"Yes," he responded with a flickering voice. "God forgive you as I forgive you, too." Instead of taming the young cannibal, the greatness of the priest's soul infuriated him tremendously.

"God forgive us?" the German asked sarcastically. "Then whatever you do, you have nothing to fear. Go to hell." And he hit him vehemently with a bayonet, holding the eyes of the vulnerable priest. The priest fell on his knees at the feet of the executioner.

The tragic priest remained motionless for several minutes. Suddenly he leaned in a bit from the right side, breathing heavily. His soul was saying it would not leave him yet. The Germans saw that he still lived, so they decided to execute him once and for all. With difficulty, they put him to stand against the trunk of a tree, barely conscious. But he had a burst of life. Panagiotis Charalambopoulos let out a deep sigh and rolled in the dirt, dead.[37]

[37]Φιλοποιμην Π. Βλαγκοπουλοσ, Το Παγκρατι, Μια μικρη περιληψη της ιστορικης του διαδρομης 1687–2007; Εκδοση Συλλογου Παγκρατιωτων Καλαβρυτινων, Ο Αγιοσ Ιωαννησ Ο Θεολογοσ, Αθηνα: 2008. [Filopoimin P. Vlangopoulos, *The Pangrati: A Brief Summary of the Historical Course 1687–2007*, Kalavryta Pangratian Association, Saint

Profound Effects of World War II on the Village of Pangrati

World War II had a profound effect on the village of Pangrati and the entire region around the village. The region is commonly referred to as Kalavryta. The actual village of Kalavryta is what in the United States is called the county seat; that is, the main government offices of the region were located there. For centuries Kalavryta was the location of the central government for the region.

The war in Greece started out peaceful enough. The fighting was in northern Europe and was only of passing interest in the remote mountains of the Peloponnese. The local residents had their own problems coping with the difficult living conditions. Survival was hard work. They had their hands full trying to get their crops to grow. Mild weather was needed to get the best possible harvest. They were not rich by any measure. They were living day-to-day, taking their goats and sheep to pasture to graze. They would milk the goats and make delicious cheese, known to the world now as feta.

They grew olives, dates, figs, grapes and walnuts. These crops gave them much needed nourishment and something to trade for blankets or yarn so they could make blankets for their families, since it gets quite cold at night in the winter up in the mountains. Thieves took whatever they could from others to feed themselves and their families. It wasn't all wine and roses, as they say, or wine and feta. And since they all lived in small

John the Theologist, Athens: 2008 (as translated from Greek by Theodore P. Georgas).]

villages like Pangrati, everyone knew everyone else. They knew each person's reputation and personality like they knew themselves.

While the village was like a big extended family, each village had its share of despicable people. Over the years various villages would have minor skirmishes with neighboring villages. There were always issues and controversies festering among the Greeks in the region. There was talk of the war, but of more import to the locals was the infiltration in the area of influences from people that came to the area from faraway places. Many of these outsiders told them about socialism and the ways of communism. They said that in their homelands things were so much different. These communistic ideas appealed to some local Greeks. The socialistic idea of everyone working together for a common good sounded wonderful. Others thought of these systems as a chance to better themselves or to use such philosophical ideals to influence others. Some people could gain power in this type of system—power and wealth were desired by a small fraction of the population. This talk would have a powerful influence on events that took place in the region throughout World War II and beyond for decades. This really came to light during the years of the Greek Civil War, which took place as an internal struggle for control of the country during World War II and afterwards until 1949. Even today, major political differences still burn in the hearts of Greeks as a result of treaties from earlier times.

The Greeks really didn't trust anybody. They had been living under suppression by the Turks for nearly 400 years, and when they saw the Germans, Austrians and Italians attacking foreign countries they dreaded fighting those powerful armies. Before the Turks, the Greeks were under the rule of the Franks, the Romans and the Macedonians. And after the Turks, the Venetians ruled them. But throughout the two millennia of suppression they learned how to survive as a people. Largely, they used the Church and the Greek Orthodox religion to keep themselves together through thick and thin.

Numerous times the Greeks rose up to fight their suppressors. Here is an example, written by Hermann Frank Meyer.[38]

> "In a series of uprisings that at times took on widespread bellicose proportions, the enslaved Hellenes fought against the hated oppressor. And this was countered with means that were beyond all legal norms: for centuries, the Hellenes were exterminated, tortured and burned.
>
> To escape Turkish arbitrariness, the young men fled to the mountains, from where they took up the fight against the usurpers. In songs and rhymes, the brave Andartes were called "pallikaria" (heroes) or "klephten" (robbers) as they attacked from a safe mountain led by a "kapetanios." The Turkish occupiers, throughout the centuries, despite extensive undertakings and terrible punitive expeditions, never succeeded in putting the insurgents to work.
>
> Eight years of war led to the liberation of Greece in 1829. No wonder, then, that the Kalavrytan monastery of Agia Lavra is worshiped by all Greek

[38] Meyer, *From Vienna to Kalavryta* (translated from the German by Theodore P. Georgas).

patriots as a national shrine. And it is a must of every Greek to visit the mountain town with its famous monastery once in their lifetime." [39]

It was no surprise that when the Italians invaded Greece, the Greeks once again turned to their old methods of survival. In no place was this more powerful than right in the mountains of the Peloponnese known as the Kalavryta area.

The Greeks knew how to pretend to be friends with the invaders but then to steal from them in any way they could. When the Italians came into the Kalavryta region, shrewd Greeks welcomed them with open arms. The Italians at first thought the Greeks were sincerely friendly, but over time they learned that not all Greeks were truly to be trusted. And the Italian army had great needs themselves, which required them to take much away from the Greeks. They had to feed themselves, so they took the goats and sheep away from the Greeks. They needed places to sleep, so they took over the towns. The leaders of the Italian army took over the best houses in each village during the occupation. Nobody knew how long this would last. These were very difficult arrangements to live through. The Greeks felt like they were prisoners in their own villages and homes.

My great-grandmother, Costantina Georgakopoulou, was a rather wealthy Pangrati resident, so when the Italians came to her village, they would no doubt look to her and wonder if she were involved in providing money, weapons, food and other supplies to the Greek rebels that were causing them issues. *Issues* might be too soft a word: Italian soldiers out on patrol

---

[39] Meyer, *From Vienna to Kalavryta* (translated from the German by Theodore P. Georgas).

would frequently be shot at, captured, harassed or robbed by small groups of Greek rebels known as Andartes. Perhaps that was why the Italians burned the village of Pangrati to the ground in the summer of 1943. It was not the last time the village would be destroyed during the war. In fact, over the next year it would be burned three more times by the German army.

After the Italian army left the region and were replaced by the Germans, the local Greeks were once again outwardly friendly to the invaders, but many were secretly doing whatever they could to undermine the German army and their war efforts. The Greeks, who had survived centuries of oppression, were not going to sit idly by and let the Germans rule them. The Kalavrytans were also happy to take the advice, weapons, supplies and money offered to them by the Russians (communists) that infiltrated the area. They were equally willing to accept the same things from the British military advisors that were dropped into the area by the Allied forces. Because of the weapons and ammunition they stole from the Italian army, the Russians and the British, the Greeks thought they could do something really important and impactful to make a difference in the war and save their villages, the Kalavryta region, the Peloponnese, and perhaps even all of Greece. But how and where this would happen no one knew.

They got great pleasure from little incidents that disrupted the enemy, but this displayed their local heroism rather than making a big impact on the war. But with encouragement from the Russians, the British and the Greek church leaders, they kept it up. This effort had a bigger impact on the Germans than they thought—word got all the way back to German headquarters and to Hitler himself that things were behind schedule in southern Greece. This greatly infuriated him.

Hitler had wanted the entire Peloponnese to be firmly under German control for two reasons that were of vital importance to his overall goals of defeating all the Allied countries and their militaries. The first reason was that he had enormous armies fighting all over Europe and Africa, and these armies needed huge amounts of supplies, which had to be constantly delivered. Without the needed supplies his armies would be useless. After all, how could they fight without ammunition, weapons, boots or food? Hitler wanted a road network that ran basically straight south through Greece to the Mediterranean Sea. From there he could disperse supplies to Africa or Russia as needed. Every time the local Greeks ripped up a road or destroyed a bridge it delayed the completion of the German highway and thus caused Hitler great anguish. He was constantly replacing commanders that couldn't meet his demands or schedules.

The second reason Hitler wanted the Peloponnese completely secured was that he thought Allied forces led by the United States would invade southern Greece and then march straight up Greece into Austria and into Germany. Hitler could not accept fighting the Allies on a southern front, since he was already fighting them to his west, to the east and in Africa as well.

The news of how the Allies gained ground in several places worried Hitler to no end. He wanted total submission by the Greeks in the Peloponnese. While he was having much success in most of the Peloponnese, his forces were not able to really control the mountains in and around the Kalavryta area, including Pangrati. The Greek Andartes were too elusive. Every time the Germans went out on their long patrols to try to capture and control the Andartes they would fail, for the Greeks knew far in advance when the Germans were coming to an area or a village. So usually when the Germans arrived at a village there would be no residents there. They would all be hiding in the mountains, the forests, the hills or sometimes caves.

In addition, the German patrols were too small to really surround any area or village, as the region was huge. The Germans would loudly enter the village from one direction, giving the residents ample time and three other directions to escape. The Germans would go from village to village looking for suspected Andartes or communists, also known as ELAS. They would kill anyone they thought was an enemy or any they thought might be helping the Andartes. They routinely burned down the houses of the Andartes families. They would first take all the possessions from the properties of the Andartes and their friends and family. This was still not enough to deter the Andartes. In fact, the Andartes were getting stronger and gaining more and more recruits. After they captured a couple of German soldiers the incident would become famous in the region, and everyone wanted to join that kind of group. Oftentimes the Andartes had to turn away boys that were too young to join.

A major event happened as the Germans tried to put an end to the Andartes once and for all. They were going to sweep through the region where the rebels were believed to be the strongest and kill or capture them. So, on October 16, 1943, they came on a 10-hour march from the Aigio and Diakopto camps south toward Kalavryta. They marched through the villages of Zevgolatio, Nikoleika, Derveni, Mamousia, Doumena and Rogoi.

The Germans were poorly led by Captain Hauptmann Schober. Schober seemed to be more in a hurry to reach his destination than to follow good military practices. He was planning on talking to the Greeks to find out where the enemy was and didn't really think that his group of 97 soldiers would be attacked. For instance, he told his men to carry only the bare minimum of supplies and equipment so they could move more quickly across the mountains. It was decided to give each soldier only 100 rounds of ammunition for his rifle. They had minimal rations and only a single canteen of water per man. They also decided not to carry heavy weapons, such as

Approximate route traveled by the Hauptmann Schober Group. Map created using google Maps.

grenade launchers or machine guns, since they were not bringing any pack animals to help carry the load. And probably Schober's biggest mistake was to not bring any walkie-talkies, so he had no way to call for reinforcements if he needed help. The soldiers also marched in a poorly formed formation that would have been easy to attack. They were all packed closely together instead of in a longer formation that would be more difficult to ambush.

When the Germans got to Rogoi, they stopped to rest briefly and refill their canteens in the creek. They were close to their planned location for the night, Kerpini. The Greeks had been following them all day and watching them closely. When the Germans stopped in a clearing that was rather bowl shaped the Greeks knew they could nearly surround the Germans and shoot at them from the higher, more protected ground. The Andartes-led Nikitas took up positions on three sides of the Germans. When the Germans started moving up a slope of vineyards toward Kerpini, the Greeks started firing upon them from the front and two sides, just after the bells of Kerpini began to ring.

The Germans had come across a large group of Andartes that managed to pin them down. A battle raged there for the rest of the day and into the night. The Germans would eventually run out of ammunition and were forced to surrender to the Greeks. Only four Germans were killed in the battle, and three had been badly wounded. The Greeks took the wounded Germans to Kerpini, then moved them to Kalavryta and then again to Mazeika (now known as Kleitoria). A few Germans escaped, and the rest became prisoners of the Greeks.

In any case, the Kalavrytans now faced a much more serious problem caused by the Andartes, and that, according to school inspector Papavassiliou, played a major role in the impending disaster. There were two young men from the neighboring village of Soudena, the same village from which 18-year-old high school student Konstantinos Pavlopoulos had come. Pavlopoulos had been hanged by the German tank hunter group in Kalavryta on September 1st. In retaliation, the two Soudena men eventually killed the three wounded German soldiers who had been taken to the Kalavrytan hospital after the Kerpini battle.

It is true that the three wounded soldiers had been cared for by the sisters and doctors at the hospital, especially Father Hampsas, but at daybreak on October 18, the ELAS/Andartes persisted in their plan to abduct them. Dr. Pavlopoulos, who was a distant relative of the murdered high school student, insisted that the three wounded Germans leave Kalavryta, accompanied by relatives and friends of the hanged man.

Dr. Hampsas, the hospital staff, school inspector Papavassiliou and dignitaries, and even the ELAS kapetanios Kolokotronis advocated leaving the wounded in the hands of the Kalavrytan medical team. Despite heated debate, they could not prevent Dr. Pavlopoulos from taking the wounded men. The young Germans, feeling their end approaching, cried when the sisters took them out of their beds and handed them over to the avengers of the hanged high school student.

The next day, the three wounded Germans were found in a waterhole about 20 minutes south of Kalavryta. Their skulls had been smashed with a sharp object, presumably a pickaxe, and their bodies thrown into the hole.[40]

The Germans would eventually discover the bodies of these three men at the bottom of the well, their bodies mutilated because of pent-up anger in the revenge-minded Greeks. This discovery infuriated the German soldiers and their leaders. They

---

[40] Meyer, *From Vienna to Kalavryta* (translated from the German by Theodore P. Georgas).

themselves wanted revenge on the Greeks that had so heinously killed their fellow countrymen.

German Atrocities in 1943

According to official German documents, Unternehmen Kalavryta ("Operation Kalavryta") was put into effect at the beginning of December 1943. Coordinated German units left their bases in Megalópoli–Tripoli, Patra, Aigio and Argos, organized in company-sized units for the operation against the "gangs" and for the search and recovery of the prisoners. Their mission was to encircle the mountainous area around Kalavryta, rid it of Andartes, free the prisoners who had been taken in the Battle of Kerpini, and search for any weapons and propaganda materials. In that operation, the German Schutzstaffel (SS; Protection Squadron), acting independently, also participated, without reporting to the regular army. The German units were split into three groups: one was headed to the Kerpini– Zachlorou–Rogoi region, led by the new commander, Major Ebersberger; another, led by Captain Gnass, moved toward the east side of Mount Helmos to prevent the Andartes from escaping toward Korinthos; and the third, led by Major Kockert, passed through Mazeika and went directly to Mazi, searching for the prisoners.[41]

On December 5, 1943, the German column from the east, headed toward Mazeika, encountered minor resistance in Pangrati, where one German was killed and one wounded. In reprisal, most houses in Pangrati were destroyed, and all the men who had not run away were caught there and executed.[42]

---

[41] Peter N. Demopoulos, *Kalavryta: Occupation of 1941–1944 and the Holocaust of December 13, 1943, Memories from the Village of Aghios Nikolaos*, Hellenic University Club of Southern California, Los Angeles: 2017.
http://www.huc.org/publications/Kalavryta_Holocaust_Demopoulos_En_040717.pdf
[42] Demopoulos, *Kalavryta*.

The Germans reported hitting the village of Pangrati first on their December sweep through the area in their quest to get rid of the Andartes. At that time there were approximately 750 recorded residents of the village. Although only seven were killed on December 5th (Table 1), this was not the first time the

Table 1. German atrocities in December 1943 in and around Kalavryta

Site of shooting	Date	Number of victims
Pangrati	5	7
Lapanagous	8	5
Planitero	8	4
Rogoi	8	58
Kerpini	8	37
Near Kerpini	8	5
Ano Zachlorou	8	8
Kato Zachlorou	8	13
Mega Spilaio	8	22
Majerou	9	11
Kalavryta and Vrachni	10, 13, 14	486
Agia Lavra	14	5
Mazeika	14	8
Psari, Asprokampos	15	7

Source: Meyer, From Vienna to Kalavryta.

Germans and before them the Italians had raided and destroyed the village. Nor was it the last. I estimate that most of the men in the village were either Andartes themselves or were helping the men who were fighting the Germans and before them the Italian army. Of the 750 Pangrati residents, about 250 were men the right age to be Resistance fighters. Boys under 13 years old were not recruited as fighters but would be used for other tasks to support the Resistance. Also, men over 60 would not be involved in the fighting but would help in whatever way they could. I estimate that there were 3000–4000 Andartes in the region that were determined to deter and destroy the Axis armies that had invaded their country.

Since the German army and before them the Italians regularly moved troops and supplies from Mazeika to Tripoli and vice versa, they were constantly going right through the Pangrati area. They had set up headquarters in Tripoli to the south and Mazeika to the north. The Italian troops frequently walked through the village and interrogated people on the spot or took them back to their headquarters in nearby (6 miles [almost 10 km]) Mazeika. There, in the large house that the Italian commander had taken from the Greek owner, the Italian commanders would torture the Greeks until they gave them some information about the Andartes. Stories were told of people being made to stand at the top of the stairs and questioned. If the commander did not like the answers, he would push the person violently down the stairs. This was repeated until the person gave answers that they wanted to hear. The Greeks would be forced to tell them something or continue being tortured. It was a no-win scenario, so people often gave the commander information on their fellow Greeks. Of course, this meant that the Greeks that got reported on would have a death sentence put upon them.

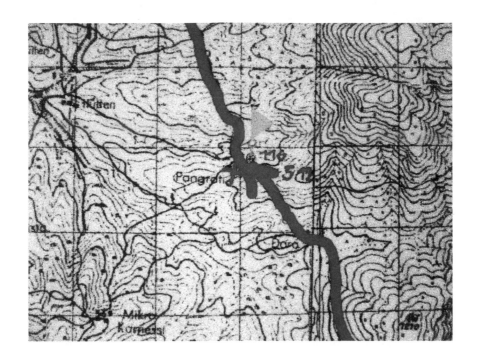

The path the German army took went right through Pangrati.
The "5 12" on the map refers to the December 5, 1943, atrocities.
Source: Courtesy of the Municipal Museum of the Kalavrytan Holocaust.

The Italians would track down the people they suspected were Andartes or helpers of the Resistance and shoot them on the spot. No trials took place, just instant reprisals. Other people recalled years later seeing the village of Pangrati burned to the ground by the German forces. The Germans did this three times; the first was on November 5, 1943. They came to the village that day and questioned everyone they thought might give them information on the Andartes. They would ask for the important people of the village, such as the doctor, the priest or the mayor. They would torture these people if they came forward. But mostly the Greeks could hear and see the Germans coming at least 30 minutes prior to their arrival. The Greeks would flee the village and go higher up the mountain and hide in caves or forests—wherever they couldn't be seen by the Germans. A few people would stay behind in the village, usually young children with their mothers and the older people.

*The remains of the house of my great-grandmother
Costantina Georgakopoulou 1960.*

My great-grandmother Costantina Georgakopoulou was a prominent person in the village and did not leave when the Germans came. She was rather elderly, nearly 80 years old, and could not run up the mountains to hide. She had a large two-story home, and on one occasion, on November 5, 1943, was upstairs sleeping or baking bread at the time, or both. I have heard different versions of the story. The Germans came to her house and set it on fire. She woke up and ran out of the house, but then ran back inside to get the bread she had just baked or some other valuables. Keep in mind a loaf of bread was very valuable in those times. A loaf that had cost 10 drachmas before the war was worth about 200,000 drachmas by 1944. This decision to rescue her valuables cost her her life. She would survive her burns for 10 days until she expired. She was just one of thousands that were killed by the German army.

The Germans would come back a month later on December 5th and burn the village again, as well as shoot those they thought were Andartes or Resistance sympathizers. The last reported burning down of the village would come in July of 1944, just a month before the Germans withdrew from Greece.

I've been told a family story about one of the times the Germans came to destroy the village. My relatives were hiding in a nearby cave to save themselves from the horrors that the Germans would inflict on anyone they encountered. My dad's aunt was with her small boy (about one year old), a cousin of my dad. The villagers were hiding in the cave when the German troops traveled nearby. The little boy started to cry. The people in the cave were terrified the German soldiers would hear the sobbing and kill them all. One of the men said they needed to kill the boy to save the rest of them. This was not a pleasant idea to any of them, but what could they do? They had to act quickly to save themselves. Then one of the others said perhaps the boy was just hungry or thirsty. But they had nothing with them for him to eat or drink. One of the men urinated in a cup and handed it to the boy's mother, who fed the urine to her boy. It worked. The boy stopped crying, and the Germans never found them. My relatives lived for another day, which was about all they could hope for. That boy would grow up and move to the United States. He went into the restaurant business with his brothers, and they were very successful. He would also marry and have a family. Therefore, it was a blessing that they hadn't killed the boy at that horrifying time in their lives.

There was an area that stretched about 20 miles (32 km) from Kalavryta on the north to Pangrati on the south. This area was involved in the Resistance uprising that was causing the Germans much turmoil during their operations in the northern Peloponnese. About 15 villages were actively involved in this movement to hinder the German army. All these villages would suffer tremendously during the war, especially from the autumn of 1943 through July 1944. The aftermath of the war left the region devoid of all the things that one would need to live. Houses were destroyed, crops ruined, livestock killed, rivers polluted, trees picked clean of any fruit, and roads and bridges destroyed. The stench of death was everywhere. Diseases were easy to catch but difficult to cure.

All of these villages saw huge drops in their population as a result, but no village was more devastated than Pangrati. The population fell from 740 in 1941 to 63 in 2011, a 91 percent loss. And the village had already had big losses before the war, from a population near 2000 at the start of the 20th century. However, most of these losses in Pangrati happened after 1951, when the official census still had 756 residents living there. Since not too many residents of the village died in the war, where did the population go? Why did so many flee the village? The main reason was that life was extremely hard there. Food and shelter were hard to come by. The United Nations provided some short-term aid to Greece after the war, but this did not last long, as most of Europe was in shambles and assistance was needed everywhere. The Germans were pressed to pay war reparations, but they were broke, and Greece never really got much compensation. To this day the Greeks are still trying to get compensation for the destruction done to their country. And the little village of Pangrati is not the first place world leaders think of when money and other aid are handed out.

Pangrati Population		
Year	Pangrati	Pangrati with it's 3 suburbs
1834	368*	368*
1879	637	637
1896	727	727
1907	614	614
1920	678	678
1928	757	757
1940	740	740
1951	756	756
1961	407	650
1971	260	456
1981	219	393
1991	207	372
2001	150	307
2011	62	143

Three suburbs are: Pagrateika Kalyvia, Stella & Steno.
* Derived from 69 families in the French Census times 5.34 members per family which was the aveage family size at that time.[43]

The general attitude of the Greeks and the helplessness of the British can be summed up by the following: [44]

Originally there was euphoria, as the Andartes were patriots and battling for the liberation of Greece and were well received by

---

[43] EXPÉDITION Scientifique DE MORÉE. SECTION DES SCIENCES PHYSIQUES, TOME II. - 1." PARTIE GEOGRAPHIE. PAR PARIS Chez. F. G. Lavrault, impeimur-libraire, STRASBORG 1834
[44] Meyer, *From Vienna to Kalavryta* (translated from the German by Theodore P. Georgas).

the villagers. The villages supplied them with food and other necessities, but after a while their devotion to the Andartes ebbed. Roughly 30 percent of the villages' populations belonged to the Andartes, but half of them had joined it only for purely opportunist reasons.

The villagers bitterly realized that their freedom fighters, because of inadequate training and leadership, would rarely seriously distress the occupier, apart from some random terrorist attacks.

After firing a few rounds from far away, with the safe mountains behind them, the Andartes sat down while the civilians that stayed in the villages were exposed to the occupier's murderous revenge.

Along with the forced recruitment of the village youth by the EAM/Andartes, the villagers were forced to provide food. Purchasing food, however, was hardly possible due to the enormous inflation rate. Whereas a gold pound was exchanged for about 200,000 drachmas in July 1943, an increase of 400 percent from 1939, the exchange rate exploded in the spring of 1944. In March 1944 it was 8 million drachmas; in April, 37 million; in May, 195 million; and in July, 288 million.

In the face of this currency devaluation, the impoverished population reverted to an archaic barter system that utilized mainly only olive oil, beans and bread. To make matters worse, the olive harvest of 1943 was the worst in years, due to adverse weather conditions. Since the price of wheat had also become prohibitive, the most important food, bread, was made from a mixture of barley and corn, and more and more often oatmeal and nuts. This diet was supplemented from time to time by a handful of beans or lentils, rarely a piece of feta cheese and greens.

The population suffered from chronic gastric complaints and ulcers, malnutrition and typhus epidemics, especially since the hygiene in the villages mocked every description. Clothes were perforated rags. Good footwear was rare. Even cooking pots and other household appliances had to be shared by several families. When night fell, there was no oil for the lamps, so an endlessly dark and scary night followed.

In the face of this misery and the approaching winter, the British provided 2000 gold pounds so the EAM/Andartes could purchase food. However, these funds never made it to the fighting force, let alone the village population; instead, the money disappeared into dark channels.

Later, on his return to Cairo, British Colonel John Melior Stevens described in moving words the yoke under which the Greek villages suffered during the long years of occupation: [45]

> "They have suffered more than the towns during this winter [1943–44], chiefly because there are few villages in the Peloponnese which have not been visited by Andartes and Germans, often three or four times by each. As a general rule the Germans looted the houses which they found empty on their drives. The Andartes beat, looted and sent off to concentration camps those villagers who stayed behind to protect their property when the Germans came. The result is indescribable

---

[45] Meyer, *From Vienna to Kalavryta* (translated from the German by Theodore P. Georgas).

misery. Most of the winter food reserves were looted by one side or the other. All the village valuables were buried. Almost every village has had several houses burnt and the remaining ones were bare of food and furniture.

In addition, the Andarte and German prohibition of movement from the mountains to the plains, and vice versa, had prevented many villagers who normally have their fields on the plain and their flocks in the hills from collecting food from their reserves in the plains or from getting the benefit of Red Cross supplies."

According to Hermann Frank Meyer in his book *From Vienna to Kalavryta* (as interpreted from the German by Theodore P. Georgas): [46]

Forty-one British Special Operations Executive (SOE) Cairo and 17 Greek operatives in the Peloponnese were deployed by the SOE Cairo headquarters. From mid-October 1943 on, they limited themselves almost exclusively to military intelligence—collecting news, espionage—and distributing relief supplies. Fruitful cooperation with the EAM/ELAS did not happen after the elimination of the Greek Army. As the British later self-critically expressed, they had done nothing productive until the withdrawal of the Germans from the Peloponnese, when they destroyed a

---

[46] Meyer, *From Vienna to Kalavryta* (translated from the German by Theodore P. Georgas).

railway bridge north of Kyparissia, which had been rebuilt after two weeks. The result was two militarily meaningless terrorist attacks on Argos. The cost was the lives of many innocent and their total isolation from the only remaining Resistance organization of the peninsula. After his return to Cairo in June 1944, Stevens criticized himself, saying that he had probably forfeited his ability to function as a British liaison officer (BLO).

Accusations were also made by the British, who felt that their activities had left countless Greek patriots dead. In the collection of military data, the BLOs relied predominantly on the statements of more prudent forces, such as clergy, former mayors and teachers. The sole aim of those men was to protect the civilian population from revenge by the occupier and, as much as possible, to stay out of the dreadful war events as V-men in the service of the Germans.

Both the British and the Germans complained about the sudden disappearance of their agents. The BLO Captain Gibson, for example, reported that he had to stop his espionage activity because all his contacts had disappeared. In plain language, this means that these men had been murdered by the EAM/ELAS or ill-treated, or at best they had fled.

Abandoned by the British and persecuted by the ELAS, Greek Army Andarte Colonel Dionysios Papadongonas, once again sought dialog with the Germans, which at the end of the year would lead to the deployment of the notorious Greek security regiments. Together with the Wehrmacht and SS associations, these were to be fierce battles with the ELAS until the end of the war. The testimony to this is a first firefight between the so-called Nationals and the so-called communists on November 11: the Nationals captured 12 prisoners and handed them over to the German Wehrmacht and thus to certain death.[47]

At the time of these horrible events in Pangrati, far away in the United States my grandparents, who had been born and raised in the village, heard through letters from their brothers and sisters back home how bad things were in Greece. It must have been very difficult for them to hear how their own flesh and blood were suffering so incredibly. My grandmother, Veneta Vlagos Georgas, and her husband, my grandfather, Theodore Nicholas Georgas, wanted to get her relatives out of the horrible place that had been her home and bring them safely to the United States. It would take her years, but she made good on her promise. Veneta's uncle, John Vlagos Raklios, had sponsored her migration to the United States in 1922. She realized that he had saved her from the horrors that transpired in her village and in the region during World War II and, even after that, during the Greek Civil War. So she helped her brothers and their families come to the United States. She helped them get jobs and housing and simply did everything that she could do to help them out.

---

[47] Meyer, *From Vienna to Kalavryta* (translated from the German by Theodore P. Georgas).

Aerial view of the village of Pangrati. Source: Google Earth 2013.

Other Interesting Facts about Pangrati

According to my cousin Veneta Vlangos Usechek (who is named after my grandmother), until the 1960s in the village of Pangrati there was

- no electricity,
- no running water,
- no employment,
- no telephone,
- no radio, and
- no doctors.

While there was no running water in the village until the 1960s, I do know that my great-grandmother Costantina Georgakopoulou was the first person in the village to have a water well, which had to be before she died in 1943/4.

Veneta Vlangos Usechek was only three years old when in 1958 her family was finally able to get out of their home village of Pangrati and immigrate to the USA. Her father, Gust Vlangos had left the village three years earlier and came to the USA to start a new life and escape the misery of life in the village. He was helped greatly by his sister, Veneta Vlagos Georgas, my grandmother and her husband Theodore N. Georgas my grandfather. They did everything they could to get Gust settled and found him a job and even helped him buy a house in Wheaton, Illinois, which is where they lived along with my aunt Connie and her husband Gus Kosiara and my family. I was only two years old at the time that the Gust Vlangos family arrived, but I do remember them coming to my grandparents' house since they lived right next to our house. I was surprised at how they looked because no one else in Wheaton looked like them, not even my Greek relatives. Their appearance was of thin build and they wore shabby clothes. But they were full of life and looking forward to their new home and life in the USA even though they always thought about their true home as being Pangrati.

Like so many others they needed to leave their little village to find a better life and the Pangratians would end up all over the world in places far away such as Argentina, Australia, and the United States of America.

Traditions/Customs of the Pangrati

Pangrati, like most villages in Greece, has had many traditions, especially back in the times when it had a larger population. The following describe some of the more important rituals. The Greeks brought many of these practices with them when they migrated to the United States and other countries.

Christmas

Christmas is very deeply engraved in the faith of the Christian tradition and cultural heritage. It is one the biggest events involving moral and religious customs; the other is Holy Easter. Christmas celebrations are known as the Twelve Day ceremony, which begins on Christmas Eve and ends with Epiphany on January 6th.

Christian homes are flooded with best wishes on Christmas Eve. Doors are open wide, particularly for children carrying the great celebration message. Messages from kids, greetings, and praise for the homeowners are also given on New Year's Eve and Epiphany. Children sing carols at each house.

In all households in the village these celebrations, particularly Christmas, are festive with joy and songs after rich meals enhanced with meats, including the traditional turkey. Families focus on respect for the elders and on the affection and love of the children. Wishes are abundant, and there is much singing.

In Greek Orthodox tradition, baklava, kourabiedes, melomakarona and other traditional pastries are baked on Christmas Eve, while Christopsomo is a bread baked on

Christmas Day (it literally means "bread of Christ"). A cross is formed on the top of the bread.[48]

All of this family joy is followed by religious joy that proceeds as solemn rites of the Church. On Christmas Day, Orthodox Christians attend the divine liturgy and receive the Holy Eucharist or Holy Communion. It is traditional to light candles in honor of Jesus, the Light of the world.[49]

Another custom we still have in modern times is decorating a Christmas tree in every home. This custom has prevailed throughout Greece since the time of King Otto (king of Greece May 27, 1832 – October 23, 1862) and certainly gives a special touch to Christmas celebrations.

The celebration of the New Year has another character. Special greetings are exchanged, such as "Successful and Happy New Year." This day of celebration is related to a very old custom in which the children get gifts from Santa Claus (Saint Basil). The kids still tend to believe that Saint Basil comes from Caesarea during the night and distributes gifts to their homes.[50]

Basil of Caesarea, also called Saint Basil the Great (Ελληνική Ἅγιος Βασίλειος ὁ Μέγας, Ἅγιος Μπάσιος, AD 329 or 330–379), was the Greek bishop of Caesarea Mazaca in Cappadocia, Asia Minor (modern-day Turkey). In Greek tradition, he brings gifts to children every January 1st (Saint Basil's Day). It is traditional on Saint Basil's Day to serve vasilopita, a rich bread baked with a coin inside. It is customary on his feast day to visit the homes of

[48] St. Andrew Greek Orthodox Church, South Bend, Indiana, "Orthodox Christmas Traditions," December 13, 2012, http://saintandrewgoc.org/home/2012/12/13/orthodox-christmas-traditions.html
[49] St. Andrew, "Orthodox Christmas Traditions."
[50] Vlangopoulos, The Pangrati (as translated from the Greek by Theodore P. Georgas).

friends and relatives, to sing New Year's carols, and to set an extra place at the table for Saint Basil. Basil, born into a wealthy family, gave all his possessions to the poor, the underprivileged, those in need, and children. For Greeks and others in the Orthodox tradition, Saint Basil is the saint associated with Santa Claus, as opposed to the Western tradition of Saint Nicholas.[51]

The Cake and the Coin

By the time Saint Basil was Bishop of Caesarea in Asia Minor, a prince demanded that he surrender the treasures of the Kingdom of Cappadocia or the city would be attacked and conquered.

Saint Basil prayed all night, begging the Lord to protect and save the city. But the prince, looking forward and not caring about the treasure, immediately surrounded Caesarea and asked boldly to see the bishop, who was in the temple praying.

Basil the Great accepted the prince and highlighted the poverty and hunger of the people, who were not in possession of any treasures. Immediately, the prince began to threaten the bishop, telling him that he would be sent to exile or even to death. But the faithful people of Caesarea, who loved their bishop, gathered what they had in order to save him and their city.

Saint Basil presented the prince with the treasure trove. Before the prince approached the treasure, a great army of angels attacked and defeated the enemy troops, thus saving the city of Caesarea.

---

[51] Basil of Caesarea, https://en.wikipedia.org/wiki/Basil_of_Caesarea

But then Saint Basil was put into a very difficult situation. What should he do with the treasures, which included gold jewelry? Should it be divvied up and given back to the residents of the city? Or should everyone get back whatever they had donated? He prayed to the Lord, and the Lord gave him the solution.

He asked the bakers to prepare bread rolls and directed them to insert a few pieces of gold jewelry. Once the rolls were prepared, they were distributed as a blessing to the faithful. Everyone was surprised by this move and were even more surprised when they cut the bread and found their own gold jewelry.

This was a special bread. It became known as the New Year's cake that brought joy and blessings. Since then, to maintain the tradition, the residents of Pangrati make cake or bread and place a coin inside, on the first day of each year.

The coin hidden in the cake or bread, known as vasilopita, brings good luck for the year.[52]

Screaming Village

In the 20th century the village had a town crier that would announce the decisions of the village rulers to the entire population. The crier would make these announcements in the evening after the people had completed their functions for the day and were at home.

The church bell was rung to get the attention of all residents, who would come outside to hear the announcement. The crier would stand in a high place and very loudly make the

---

[52] Vlangopoulos, *The Pangrati* (as translated from the Greek by Theodore P. Georgas).

announcement. He would repeat it again to make sure everyone heard it. And the residents would repeat it again to each other so that everyone definitely heard the same message.

One such message was that they needed to rebuild the bridge over the river. All able-bodied residents would be expected to donate their time to help out with this community service. The old bridge had served well for the last year, but now the powerful river had overflowed its banks and damaged the old bridge to the point of it becoming useless.

The church bell was used for other things besides announcing the decisions of the rulers. It would ring twice when a village resident died. It would ring in times of war to announce that the invading armies were coming toward the village. It was used to quickly inform the residents about a multitude of things.[53]

Evil Eye

Another village superstition involved a belief in the "evil eye." The prevailing belief was that some people in the village had the magical ability to put the evil eye on other people. The evil eye may have been the perceived cause of mental illness. People known as doctors in the village used "drugs"—mostly their own herbs and inventions—to protect people from the evil eye. Garlic, for example, was considered immune to the evil eye. Coal and frankincense were also thought to be effective. These drugs were recommended as a precaution and mainly used for young children. Mothers used them as a lucky charm or amulet to protect their kids. One evil-eye doctor in particular was known throughout the region for his healing powers. It was believed

---

[53] Vlangopoulos, *The Pangrati* (as translated from the Greek by Theodore P. Georgas).

that he had the magical ability to heal those suffering from the evil eye. He was known as Uncle John. When Uncle John learned that someone in the village was sick, he immediately ran and willingly examined the person to diagnose the illness. Being kindhearted, he tied three grains of incense and three grains of salt in a handkerchief. Then he began the "crossing," while simultaneously mumbling an exorcism, which no one else ever learned. The crossing was repeated three times with a wish list, and then he declared that the sick would be well shortly. He departed, satisfied. In Pangrati, Uncle John was highly respected and loved.[54]

Funerals and Burial Traditions

The death of a loved one is never pleasant for the surviving family members, but religion and traditions play a most important role in this final aspect of a person's time on earth. Throughout the world, the rituals following death are handled according to the local religion and customs. In Pangrati the people have very strong Greek Orthodox religious beliefs and follow decades-old customs. The funeral is not like what you are accustomed to in whatever part of the world you live in, unless you live in a small village in Greece.

The funeral starts at the home of the deceased. Visitations typically take place the day and evening before the burial and serve as a time for family and friends to share stories and memories. A priest will hold a service, where he leads prayers and hymns.

---

[54] Vlangopoulos, *The Pangrati* (as translated from the Greek by Theodore P. Georgas).

The funeral procession is quiet and moves along the route to the church. The funeral itself is held in the church and includes a traditional service. Mourners are invited to pay their last respects to the deceased before the casket is transported to the cemetery for burial.

The village has very limited room in their cemetery, and burial space is very hard to come by and is expensive. Because of this, coffins are very small, and the deceased is squeezed into a space about half the size of what we in the United States are accustomed to. The casket is open; in other words, it has no lid. The caskets do not have handles protruding from the sides, which would make it easier to carry the deceased person into and out of the church and to the burial site. The pall bearers need to lift the coffin up onto their shoulders and carry the body very carefully while walking up and down hills and steps. They try to stay in step with each other so as not to drop the coffin and cause the loved one to fall out.

Once at the cemetery, the coffin is placed in the ground, and dirt is thrown into the grave. A short prayer ceremony is held, flowers are placed at the grave, and the casket is interred. Following the service, mourners visit the bereaved family to offer their condolences and partake in a makaria, a meal not unlike the one that followed a funeral in ancient Greece. The food served is rather bland fish and very garlicky potatoes.

Three days after the death, and the spirit has been released from the body, the family enters a mourning period of 40 days. This is the amount of time between Christ's resurrection and ascension. After the burial, customary church services are held in remembrance of the deceased. The first is on the Sunday nearest to 40 days after death. Subsequent memorial services are held every three months for the first year, after one year, after three years, and after seven years.

After three years the body is dug up and taken out of the casket. The bones are washed and placed into an above-ground family vault containing the bones of all the ancestors. When I visited the village in 1992 Uncle Gust Vlangos showed me and my sister the burial vault of our ancestors, which were also his ancestors. He said that he could open the vault and show us the bones of all of our relatives interred there. I told him that wasn't necessary.

My uncle Gust Vlangos and my sister Sandy at the family grave in the Pangrati cemetery in 1992.

Water Mills of Pangrati

Because of Pangrati's unique location, it made perfect sense to build mills along the rivers that were so important to everyone in the region. The Aroanios and Ladon rivers come together at the foot of the mountain where the village is located. The two rivers, along with several tributaries, all merge in and around the village.

Mills had been around in Europe for centuries. The earliest evidence of a water-driven wheel is probably the Perachora wheel (3rd century BC), in Perachora, Greece, which was near Corinth. Greek engineers invented the two main components of watermills, the waterwheel and toothed gears.

The rivers and their tributaries around Pangrati had fast-moving water because of the drop in elevation from the mountains down into the river valleys. This fast-moving water was perfect for a water mill. The water had to be moving at a high velocity and easily controlled; otherwise, the grinding operation would not work properly. Once they learned how to harness the power of the moving water, the residents of Pangrati built mills near the convergence of the two rivers. People from all over the region would bring their wheat and grains to the mill for grinding.

A water mill works by diverting a portion of the water from the stream through a flume to a huge water wheel. The force of the water's movement causes the blades of the wheel to turn, which in turn rotates an axle that drives the mill's internal gears. The gears inside the mill start to spin; these are connected to a large stone that also spins. The grains brought to the mill by farmers are put into a vat with the spinning stone, which grinds the grain into flour. The flour can then be used for a variety of purposes, such as for baking bread.

Both sides of my family were involved in the Pangrati mills. My grandfather, Theodore Georgas' mother Costantina Georgakopoulou, owned one of them. On my grandmother's side of the family, her brother Gust Vlangos worked in a mill before he emigrated to the United States in 1955.

Uncle Gust was originally named Konstantine Vlangopoulos. As a young man, Kosta, as he was probably called in Greek, worked in the family-owned mill. He ground the farmers' wheat into flour. He also ran another mill that was owned by the Askunis family (that family now has a great-grandson living in Chicago). The Vlangopoulos family would rent the mill from the Askunis family so they could run it. The Vlangopoulos family became quite poor during World War II, since times were difficult for all the villagers and their customers. During that period, the kindhearted Askunis family allowed them to pay less rent.

The mill near Pangrati that was operated by my uncle, Gust Vlangos.

In 1992 when I visited the family village of Pangrati with my sister, Sandy, our uncle Gust Vlangos gave us a personal tour of the water mill where he had worked before migrating to the United States. Because of lack of use for many years, much of the place had been overtaken by greenery, but our uncle explained how he worked the mill like it had been yesterday.

Uncle Kosta joined the Greek army in September 1937, for five months. The Greek government required two years of military service from the elder males of all families. The family paid the government a fee of 2,500 drachmas to get his enlistment reduced to only five months.

Gust Vlangos and his family survived the destruction of their village twice. In November 1943 the entire village of Pangrati was burned to the ground by the German soldiers in retaliation for the death of some of their soldiers. The second time the village was destroyed was by communist Greeks. Pangrati residents were not communists; they were loyalists. A neighboring village was communist; it supplied the communist rebels with food and weapons. When a communist rebel was killed by a Pangrati resident, the rebels retaliated by burning the village down. The entire village was destroyed for the second time in only a few years. This happened during the Greek Civil War, which started right after World War II. Gust Vlangos survived by taking his family and hiding up in the hills.

The entire milling process required hard work from all involved. In the farm fields, the wheat had to be cut down and tied together into a sheaf. Wheat bales had to be transported from the field to the distant mill, usually by mules or donkeys. They needed to travel for miles up and down hazardous mountains to get there. The grain was then threshed to separate the edible parts from the chaff. The job of the millers was difficult. The components of the mill were all very large and heavy and required precision to work properly. Once the water was allowed to go through the flume and start turning the wheel and gears, millers had to be very careful. Powerful forces and danger were everywhere.

The mills were also an informal meeting place for talk and gossip about events in the region. In times of trouble, the mills were used to supply provisions to the local Greek militant fighters. During times of war, the millers' job was even more dangerous. If they were found to be helping the militant Resistance fighters, they would likely have been killed. The millers of Pangrati were very important and provided several essential services to the local residents.

Another view of the mill near Pangrati that was operated by my uncle, Gust Vlangos. My grandmother Veneta was born in this mill.

Modern-Day Pangrati

Today Pangrati is a favored destination of tourists, fishermen and hikers. Some of the best fly fishing can be had in the two rivers and their tributaries. Hiking through hills, valleys and mountains is a good way to free your mind from the stresses of everyday life. The E4 long-distance path (hiking trail) that runs across much of Europe goes right through Pangrati.

Shopping in modern Pangrati is not like shopping in the big city of Athens or what people in the United States know as shopping. Even simple things like groceries are hard to obtain in this village in the remote mountains. In Greece, although grocery stores are called supermarkets, they are quite small compared to those in the United States. The closest supermarket to Pangrati is in the village of Levidi, about a 30-minute drive. Larger supermarkets are close to an hour away. Getting routine groceries is not an everyday occurrence, but more of a major event that is done weekly. Some items, such as fresh fish, milk and cheese, are delivered to Pangrati once a week in the summer.

Levidi also has a pharmacy (aka drugstore), where the people go for routine medicines. In case of an emergency (illness or accident), the closest hospital is an hour's drive away in Tripoli.

The nearest café, bar or restaurant would be about a 20- to 30-minute drive away in either Kleitoria or Vytina. Clothing stores are somewhat farther away, an hour or more. The closest gas stations are 20- to 30-minute drives. If your vehicle breaks down or just needs routine service, you would need to drive about 1–2 hours to find a service station.

However, if you are in need of a church, well you're in luck: within 20–30 minutes you can find 20. Every village, including Pangrati, has a church. Consequently, you could walk to church in about 1–2 minutes.

Church of St. John the Theologian in Pangrati.

Pangrati cemetery. The church is in the lower left corner.

Pangrati Village school house.

My cousin Penny Vlagos said, "Some of my relatives, such as John Vlangos, attended the school in Pangrati. They would attend the school in the village until they were old enough to go to junior high and high school. Kleitoria (Mazeika) is where the junior high and high school were located, and that is where city hall is for Pangrati—in the main square. When the kids from the village attended school in Kleitoria they used to rent a room there to go to school during the week and then on Friday evening walk for three hours back to the village to help out with chores at home. Then on Sunday night they would walk back to Kleitoria so they could attend school for the week."

Today it is a common practice to sacrifice a goat for Easter. When my parents visited Greece and the village of Pangrati back in the 1970s they happened to go during Dad's spring break from his job as a teacher. And that year spring break coincided with Easter. When they got to the village, they were fed a marvelous feast. The Greek relatives, his cousins, had killed one of their most prized possessions, their goat. It was a time of rejoicing and celebration that happens once a year in the village and throughout all of Greece.

In the village once a year there is a huge celebration that goes on for five days. It takes place every August when Greek children are out of school for the summer break. The central theme is to remember and celebrate the Dormition of Virgin Mary, the Mother of God. August 15th is her special date in the Greek Orthodox Church which means it is one of the biggest holidays in Greece. The observances take place throughout the entire country of Greece. The City of Athens empties out as most Greeks travel back to their ancestral villages for the festivities. For my relatives that means a trip to stay in and around Pangrati. The village doesn't have enough beds in it for everyone, so people fill up the hotels in the nearby towns, such as Kleitoria. For the 2019 celebration, which was the 25th annual event, 400 people attended the festivities in Pangrati. The activities at the festival include numerous competitions for the children to try their luck. The contests go on for days and include singing, painting, musical chairs, fishing, dancing, foot races, mini golf, and basketball three-point shooting. Dozens of kids win events and get recognized. The celebration of course included terrific tasting foods prepared by dedicated Pangratians. Some of the attendees come from far away countries such as Australia, Canada, Cyprus, Germany and the USA.

Pausanias (ca. AD 110–180) was the travel writer and geographer who visited Pangrati in the second century. The legend told for many generations is that he sat under this vine in Pangrati on his travels from Mantineia. He wrote 10 travel books while he was roaming around Greece, the first travel guides ever written. The vine of Pausanias has a huge trunk and branches that spread over a large area in the churchyard of Saint Nicholas in Pangrati. In a book on Arcadia, Pausanias mentions the vine as a peculiar phenomenon. Its age is estimated to be 3000 years. Every year in May it blossoms, but it never has any fruit.

Vine tree of Pausanias.

The village of Pangrati begun in the times of the Greek gods, Zeus and Apollo. The vine of Pausanias may have been a Dryad, a tree nymph, perhaps it was Erato herself, the mother of the mythical king Azan. From ancient days to today Pangrati has been an important part of not just Greek but also world history.

References

"Basil of Caesarea." https://en.wikipedia.org/wiki/Basil_of_Caesarea

Demopoulos, Peter N. *Kalavryta: Occupation of 1941–1944 and the Holocaust of December 13, 1943. Memories from the Village of Aghios Nikolaos*. Hellenic University Club of Southern California, Los Angeles: 2017. http://www.huc.org/publications/Kalavryta_Holocaust_Demopoulos_En_040717.pdf

EXPÉDITION Scientifique DE MORÉE. SECTION DES SCIENCES PHYSIQUES, TOME II. - 1." PARTIE GEOGRAPHIE. PAR PARIS Chez. F. G. Lavrault, impeimur-libraire, STRASBORG 1834

Foundation for Information on World War Two. "Deutsches Kreuz in Gold." *Traces of War*. https://www.tracesofwar.com/awards/614/Deutsches-Kreuz-in-Gold.htm?sort=name&show=list&abc=P&page=2

Municipality of Kalavryta official website. http://www.kalavrita.gr/information/istoria/item/809-to-olokaytoma-ton-kalavryton

Karasavvas, Theodoros. "Pankration: A Deadly Martial Art Form from Ancient Greece." *Ancient Origins: Reconstructing the Story of Humanity's Past*, January 23, 2016. http://www.ancient-origins.net/history-ancient-traditions/pankration-deadly-martial-art-form-ancient-greece-005221

Katsirodis, Popis. The speech of lawyer Popis Katsirodis at a memorial event in Skepasto, November 27, 2017. From the Municipality of Kalavryton. http://www.kalavrita.gr/nomika/dmko/item/1682-edilosi-mnimis-sto-skepasto-omilia-dikigorou-popis-katsirodi [As translated from the Greek by Theodore P. Georgas.]

Meyer, Hermann Frank. *Von Wien nach Kalavryta: Die blutige Spur der 117, Jäger-Division durch Serbien und Greichenland*. Mannheim: Peleus, 2002. [*From Vienna to Kalavryta: The Bloodstained Trail of the 117th Jaeger Division through Serbia and Greece*, referred to herein as *From Vienna to Kalavryta* in the footnotes. As translated from the German by Theodore P. Georgas.]

Municipal Museum of the Kalavritan Holocaust.
https://www.dmko.gr/en/

O'Donnell, Conal. "SOE, the Irish Agent and the Greek Massacre." *WW2 People's War.*
http://www.bbc.co.uk/history/ww2peopleswar/stories/37/a3206837.shtml

Pausanias's Description of Greece: *Commentary on books VI-VIII: Elis, Achaia, Arcadia;* Macmillan, 1898 - Greece

Rodgers, Nigel. *The Illustrated Encyclopedia of Ancient Greece: An Authoritative Account of Greek Military and Political Power, Architecture, Sculpture, Art, Drama and Philosophy.* Leicester: Anness Publishing: 2017.

Vlangopoulos, Filopoimin P. Το Παγκρατι, Μια μικρη περιληψη της ιστορικης του διαδρομης 1687–2007; by Φιλοποιμην Π. Βλαγκοπουλοσ, Εκδοση Συλλογου Παγκρατιωτων Καλαβρυτινων, Ο Αγιοσ Ιωαννησ Ο Θεολογοσ, Αθηνα 2008. [*The Pangrati: A Brief Summary of the Historical Course 1687–2007.* Kalavryta Pangratian Association, Saint John the Theologist, Athens: 2008. As translated from the Greek by Theodore P. Georgas.]

W.H.S. Jones Litt.D., and H.A. Ormerod, *"Pausanias. Pausanias Description of Greece with an English Translation, in 4 Volumes."* Cambridge, MA, Harvard University Press; London, William Heinemann Ltd. 1918.

Further Suggested Reading

Baedeker, Karl. *Greece Handbook for Travelers.* Leipzig: Baedeker, 1905.

Καλαβρυτα – News; *30 Δεκεμβρίου 1943 - Ο Απολογισμός της Επιχείρησης Καλάβρυτα;* Δεκεμβρίου 29, 2016. [Kalavryta - News, December 30, 1943 - *The Kalavryta Report*, December 29, 2016.] https://www.kalavrytanews.com/2016/12/30-1943.html

Kaldiri, Dimitri. Δημητρη Καλδιρη, *Το Δραμα Των Καλαβρυτων,* Εκτυπωσισ: Μ. Μανιουδακησ Επε [*The Drama of Kalavryta.* Manioudakis Ltd.]

Mazower, Mark. *Inside Hitler's Greece: The Experience of Occupation, 1941–44.* New Haven: Yale University Press, 2001.

Παγκρατεϊκα Νεα [*Pangateika News*]. http://www.kalavrytapress.gr

Varlow, Andy. *Just Another Man: A Story of the Nazi Massacre of Kalavryta, Greece.* San Rafael: Tralala Publishing, 1998.

Theodore P. Georgas has a love of history and has been his family's historian for over 26 years. In his research he has found ancestors and discovered new cousins with a variety of backgrounds and accomplishments. He has spent the last several years studying Greek history and especially delving into the Pangrati, Kalavryta region of the Peloponnese. He has become very adept at interpreting documents written in Greek, German, French and Italian. His family tree is comprised of over 10,000 individuals.

He has spent much of his research time learning about what life was like for his grand parents as they left their homeland of Greece. His grandfather was only 15 when he ran away from home and worked in the port of Patras until he could afford to pay for a trip on a ship to the USA. Why would his grandfather leave his beloved home and his family and travel halfway around the whole to a place that he knew very little about? These are the kinds of questions that drives Theodore P. Georgas, who is named after his grandfather, to strive to fully understand places such as Pangrati Greece where both of his Greek grandparents were born and raised.

Theodore is a Civil Engineer that has worked on hundreds of highway improvement projects in the Chicago Illinois region. His engineering background makes him an ardent researcher always trying to find all the detailed evidence to get the whole story. In designing a bridge over a river or highway he wanted to always make sure the bridge would be safe for generations of motorists; he also desires for his family history research to be just as detailed and accurate. The same goes for his writing of history book, such as The History of Pangrati Kalavryta, Peloponnese, Greece.

Theodore lives with his wife Mary, in Palatine, Illinois and has two adult children, Allison and Dan.

Front Cover Photo:

Picture that I took of the village of Pangrati in 1992.

Rear Cover Photo:

This is my Uncle Gust Vlangos pointing out a monument to those Pangratians that died in the wars. He showed my sister, Sandy and I the important historical sights in village of Pangrati when we visited in 1992.

The History of Pangrati Kalavryta, Greece gives a historical account of the resilient village of Pangrati and the surrounding Kalavryta region in southern Greece. The story starts by describing ancient times and progresses to the most horrific event in the history of the region, which was the holocaust committed in the city of Kalavryta in 1943, where the German occupation forces executed all of the male population and burned down the city.

Living in the village was very difficult as it was in most of Europe during the great wars. People were unemployed and starving to death. The inhabitants had to endure several invasions by numerous countries. The foreign rulers did not share the Greek culture, language or religion which the Pangratians held onto with impressive commitment. The Greeks learned to survive throughout every obstacle thrown at them.

The History of Pangrati tells the stories of heroism by the leaders of the Kalavryta community. The local priests were tortured by the Germans, but they stood fast and gave nothing to their executioners. Their suffering and dedication to their faith and community is depicted with much deserved respect.

Also described is the Battle of Pangrati in which the poor Greek farmers rose up to take on the invaders who were stealing all their money, food, equipment and livestock. The Germans responded to the Greeks by killing them with no thought of trials first in order to see who was innocent. Their orders were to kill 100 Greeks for every German soldier that was harmed.

The History of Pangrati also tells about the unique customs in the village such as Christmas celebrations, the cake and the coin, the evil eye and the screaming village. The book shows how the Greek Orthodox religion is so important to the residents that they followed these customs throughout their lives.

If you want to hear some of the amazing stories that happened in this part of the world and the profound effect that these peasant Greeks had on the entire world, then this is the book for you.

CPSIA information can be obtained
at www.ICGtesting.com
Printed in the USA
JSHW021653090120
3447JS00003B/8